"*That's my father. He's the understudy for my mother.*"

# THE NEW YORKER
## DADS 2011

**teNeues**

Published by teNeues Verlag,
Am Selder 37, 47906 Kempen, Germany,
Tel.: (02152) 916-0, Fax: (02152) 916-111,
e-mail: verlag@teneues.de,
teNeues Publishing Company,
16 West 22nd Street, New York, NY 10010, USA,
Tel: (800) 352-0305, Fax: (212) 627-9511,
teNeues Publishing UK, London
and teNeues France, Paris
**www.teneues.com**
© 2010 teNeues Verlag and teNeues Publishing Company
ISBN: 978-3-8327-**4265-2**

# THE NEW YORKER DADS

Since *The New Yorker* first appeared on newsstands, in 1925, we have seen in its pages the creation and the evolution of the one-panel cartoon. At first, the editors of the magazine simply added humorous dialogue to small illustrations depicting socialite couples, businessmen, and other ink-rendered reflections of their era. Soon, *New Yorker* illustrators began collaborating with *New Yorker* writers to create illustrations and captions that shared a common idea.

By 1930, *The New Yorker's* cartoons were internationally revered as an ingenious form of comedic commentary. Eventually, one person was doing the job of both the writer and the artist, evolving into what we call a cartoonist.

As the *New Yorker* cartoon changed, so did the way we looked at it. The very literal illustrations and captions slowly became more and more abstract. Recurring themes and topics soon became instantly recognizable to the magazine's readers. No longer did the man sitting in the chair talking to the man lying on the couch need to be identified as a psychiatrist. Readers already knew that's who he was because this was how psychiatrists were always presented in the medium. This enabled the cartoonist to emphasize the "punch line," without having to concentrate on the "setup."

Here we present some of today's most popular dad cartoons. And, if there aren't enough cartoons for you here, there are hundreds more to view free at www.cartoonbank.com, *The New Yorker's* enormous online database of cartoons, illustrations, and cover art.

THE
NEW YORKER

# Notes Notizen Notes Note Apuntes Notities

**Notes** Notizen Notes Note Apuntes Notities

# Notes Notizen Notes Note Apuntes Notities

# Notes Notizen Notes Note Apuntes Notities

# Información Personal  Persönliche Daten  **Personal Data**
## Dati Personali  Informations Personnelles  Persoonlijke Gegevens

**Name**  Name  Nom  Nome  Nombre  Naam

**Address**  Adresse  Adresse  Indirizzo  Dirección  Adres

**Tel / Mobile**

**Fax**

**E-mail**

**www**

**Company**  Firma  Société  Ditta  Compañía  Gezelschap

**Address**  Adresse  Adresse  Indirizzo  Dirección  Adres

**Tel / Mobile**

**Fax**

**E-mail**

**www**

**Notes**  Notizen  Notes  Note  Apuntes  Notities

# World Time Differences  Internationale Zeitunterschiede
## Fuseaux horaires  Fusi Orari  Diferencias De Horas Internacionales
## International Tijdsverschillen

| City | GMT | City | GMT | City | GMT |
|---|---|---|---|---|---|
| Abu Dhabi | +4 | Edinburgh | 0 | New Delhi | +5½ |
| Accra | 0 | Edmonton | -7 | New York | -5 |
| Addis Ababa | +3 | Frankfurt | +1 | Oslo | +1 |
| Alexandria | +2 | Freetown | 0 | Ottawa | -5 |
| Algiers | +1 | Geneva | +1 | Paris | +1 |
| Amman | +2 | Glasgow | 0 | Port-au-Prince | -5 |
| Amsterdam | +1 | Halifax | -4 | Prague | +1 |
| Anchorage | -9 | Harare | +2 | Pyongyang | +9 |
| Antigua (St. John's) | -4 | Havana | -5 | Rangoon | +6½ |
| Athens | +2 | Helsinki | +2 | Reykjavik | 0 |
| Atlanta | -5 | Ho Chi Minh | +7 | Rio de Janeiro | -3 |
| Auckland | +12 | Hong Kong | +8 | Riyadh | +3 |
| Azores | -1 | Honolulu | -10 | Rome | +1 |
| Baghdad | +3 | Houston | -6 | San Juan | -4 |
| Baku | +4 | Istanbul | +2 | Santiago | -4 |
| Bangkok | +7 | Jakarta | +7 | Sao Paulo | -3 |
| Barcelona | +1 | Jerusalem | +2 | Sarajevo | +1 |
| Basra | +3 | Johannesburg | +2 | Saskatchewan (Regina) | -6 |
| Beijing | +8 | Kabul | +4½ | Seoul | +9 |
| Beirut | +2 | Karachi | +5 | Shanghai | +8 |
| Belfast | 0 | Kathmandu | +5¾ | Singapore | +8 |
| Belize City | -6 | Khartoum | +3 | Sofia | +2 |
| Berlin | +1 | Kuala Lumpur | +8 | St. Louis | -6 |
| Bern | +1 | Kuwait City | +3 | St. Petersburg | +3 |
| Bogota | -5 | Lagos | +1 | Stockholm | +1 |
| Bombay | +5½ | La Paz | -4 | Sydney | +10 |
| Brussels | +1 | Lima | -5 | Taipei | +8 |
| Budapest | +1 | Lisbon | 0 | Tehran | +3½ |
| Buenos Aires | -3 | Ljubljana | +1 | Timbuktu | 0 |
| Cairo | +2 | London | 0 | Tokyo | +9 |
| Calcutta | +5½ | Los Angeles | -8 | Toronto | -5 |
| Calgary | -7 | Madrid | +1 | Tunis | +1 |
| Caracas | -4 | Managua | -6 | Ulaan Baator | +8 |
| Casablanca | 0 | Manila | +8 | Vancouver | -8 |
| Chicago | -6 | Martinique (Fort-de-France) | -4 | Vienna | +1 |
| Copenhagen | +1 | Melbourne | +10 | Vladivostok | +10 |
| Curaçao | -4 | Mexico City | -6 | Volgograd | +3 |
| Dakar | 0 | Mogadishu | +3 | Warsaw | +1 |
| Damascus | +2 | Montevideo | -3 | Winnipeg | -6 |
| Dar-es-Salaam | +3 | Montreal | -5 | Yokohama | +9 |
| Denver | -7 | Moscow | +3 | Zurich | +1 |
| Dublin | 0 | Nairobi | +3 | | |

* Please note that the above numbers are according to Winter Standard Time. For those countries which participate in Daylight Saving Time, please add one hour during the summer months.
  Time differences added/subtracted from GMT (Greenwich Mean Time).

| from \ to | (A) | (B) | (DK) | (FIN) | (F) | (D) | (GB) | (GR) | (I) | (L) | (NL) | (N) | (PL) | (P) | (E) | (S) | (CH) | (USA) |
|---|---|---|---|---|---|---|---|---|---|---|---|---|---|---|---|---|---|---|
| (A) | - | 00-32 | 00-45 | 00-358 | 00-33 | 00-49 | 00-44 | 00-30 | 00-39 | 00-352 | 00-31 | 00-47 | 00-48 | 00-351 | 00-34 | 00-46 | 00-41 | 00-1 |
| (B) | 00-43 | - | 00-45 | 00-358 | 00-33 | 00-49 | 00-44 | 00-30 | 00-39 | 00-352 | 00-31 | 00-47 | 00-48 | 00-351 | 00-34 | 00-46 | 00-41 | 00-1 |
| (DK) | 00-43 | 00-32 | - | 00-358 | 00-33 | 00-49 | 00-44 | 00-30 | 00-39 | 00-352 | 00-31 | 00-47 | 00-48 | 00-351 | 00-34 | 00-46 | 00-41 | 00-1 |
| (FIN) | 00-43 | 00-32 | 00-45 | - | 00-33 | 00-49 | 00-44 | 00-30 | 00-39 | 00-352 | 00-31 | 00-47 | 00-48 | 00-351 | 00-34 | 00-46 | 00-41 | 00-1 |
| (F) | 00-43 | 00-32 | 00-45 | 00-358 | - | 00-49 | 00-44 | 00-30 | 00-39 | 00-352 | 00-31 | 00-47 | 00-48 | 00-351 | 00-34 | 00-46 | 00-41 | 00-1 |
| (D) | 00-43 | 00-32 | 00-45 | 00-358 | 00-33 | - | 00-44 | 00-30 | 00-39 | 00-352 | 00-31 | 00-47 | 00-48 | 00-351 | 00-34 | 00-46 | 00-41 | 00-1 |
| (GB) | 00-43 | 00-32 | 00-45 | 00-358 | 00-33 | 00-49 | - | 00-30 | 00-39 | 00-352 | 00-31 | 00-47 | 00-48 | 00-351 | 00-34 | 00-46 | 00-41 | 00-1 |
| (GR) | 00-43 | 00-32 | 00-45 | 00-358 | 00-33 | 00-49 | 00-44 | - | 00-39 | 00-352 | 00-31 | 00-47 | 00-48 | 00-351 | 00-34 | 00-46 | 00-41 | 00-1 |
| (I) | 00-43 | 00-32 | 00-45 | 00-358 | 00-33 | 00-49 | 00-44 | 00-30 | - | 00-352 | 00-31 | 00-47 | 00-48 | 00-351 | 00-34 | 00-46 | 00-41 | 00-1 |
| (L) | 00-43 | 00-32 | 00-45 | 00-358 | 00-33 | 00-49 | 00-44 | 00-30 | 00-39 | - | 00-31 | 00-47 | 00-48 | 00-351 | 00-34 | 00-46 | 00-41 | 00-1 |
| (NL) | 00-43 | 00-32 | 00-45 | 00-358 | 00-33 | 00-49 | 00-44 | 00-30 | 00-39 | 00-352 | - | 00-47 | 00-48 | 00-351 | 00-34 | 00-46 | 00-41 | 00-1 |
| (N) | 00-43 | 00-32 | 00-45 | 00-358 | 00-33 | 00-49 | 00-44 | 00-30 | 00-39 | 00-352 | 00-31 | - | 00-48 | 00-351 | 00-34 | 00-46 | 00-41 | 00-1 |
| (PL) | 00-43 | 00-32 | 00-45 | 00-358 | 00-33 | 00-49 | 00-44 | 00-30 | 00-39 | 00-352 | 00-31 | 00-47 | - | 00-351 | 00-34 | 00-46 | 00-41 | 00-1 |
| (P) | 00-43 | 00-32 | 00-45 | 00-358 | 00-33 | 00-49 | 00-44 | 00-30 | 00-39 | 00-352 | 00-31 | 00-47 | 00-48 | - | 00-34 | 00-46 | 00-41 | 00-1 |
| (E) | 07-43 | 07-32 | 07-45 | 07-358 | 07-33 | 07-49 | 07-44 | 07-30 | 07-39 | 07-352 | 07-31 | 07-47 | 07-48 | 07-351 | - | 07-46 | 07-41 | 07-1 |
| (S) | 009-43 | 009-32 | 009-45 | 009-358 | 009-33 | 009-49 | 009-44 | 009-30 | 009-39 | 009-352 | 009-31 | 009-47 | 009-48 | 009-351 | 009-34 | - | 009-41 | 009-1 |
| (CH) | 00-43 | 00-32 | 00-45 | 00-358 | 00-33 | 00-49 | 00-44 | 00-30 | 00-39 | 00-352 | 00-31 | 00-47 | 00-48 | 00-351 | 00-34 | 00-46 | - | 00-1 |
| (USA) | 011-43 | 011-32 | 011-45 | 011-358 | 011-33 | 011-49 | 011-44 | 011-30 | 011-39 | 011-352 | 011-31 | 011-47 | 011-48 | 011-351 | 011-34 | 011-46 | 011-41 | - |

To place an international telephone call, dial the international access code (e.g. 011 in U.S.), the country code number, and then the local number. *without guarantee

## Alphabet Phonétique  Buchstabier-Alphabet  **Phonetic Alphabet**

| | (D) | (GB) | (USA) | (F) | International (aero) | NATO |
|---|---|---|---|---|---|---|
| A | Anton | Andrew | Abel('eibel) | Alpha | Alfa | Alfa |
| Ä | Ärger | | | | | |
| B | Berta | Benjamin | Baker | Bravo | Bravo | Bravo |
| C | Cäsar | Charlie | Charlie | Charlie | Coca | |
| Ch | Charlotte | | | | | |
| D | Dora | David | Dog | Delta | Delta | Delta |
| E | Emil | Edward | Easy | Echo | Echo | Echo |
| F | Friedrich | Frederick | Fox | Fox | Foxtrott | Foxtrott |
| G | Gustav | George | George | Golf | Golf | Golf |
| H | Heinrich | Harry | How | Hotel | Hotel | Hotel |
| I | Ida | Isaac | Item | India | India | India |
| J | Julius | Jack | Jig | Juliet | Juliet | Juliet |
| K | Kaufmann | King | King | Kilo | Kilo | Kilo |
| L | Ludwig | Lucy | Love | Lima | Lima | Lima |
| M | Martha | Martha | Mike | Mike | Metro | Mike |
| N | Nordpol | Nellie | Nan | November | Nectar | November |
| O | Otto | Oliver | Oboe | Oscar | Oscar | Oscar |
| Ö | Ökonom | | (Oubou) | | | |
| P | Paula | Peter | Peter | Papa | Papa | Papa |
| Q | Quelle | Queenie | Queen | Quebec | Quebec | Quebec |
| R | Richard | Robert | Roger | Romeo | Romeo | Romeo |
| S | Samuel | Sugar | Sugar | Sierra | Sierra | Sierra |
| Sch | Schule | | | | | |
| T | Theodor | Tommy | Tara | Tango | Tango | Tango |
| U | Ulrich | Uncle | Uncle | Uniform | Union | Uniform |
| Ü | Übermut | | | | | |
| V | Viktor | Victor | Victor | Victor | Victor | Victor |
| W | Wilhelm | William | William | Whiskey | Whiskey | Whiskey |
| X | Xanthippe | Xmas | X (Eks) | Xray | Extra | X-Ray |
| Y | Ypsilon | Yellow | Yoke | Yankee | Yankee | Yankee |
| Z | Zeppelin | Zebra | Zebra | Zulu | Zulu | Zulu |

# International Hotels  Internationale Hotels  Hôtels Internationaux
# Alberghi Internazionali  Hoteles Internacionales  Internationale Hotels

## Luxury Hotels

**Hotel Astoria**  (RUS)
39 Bolshaya Morskaya Str.
190000 St. Petersburg
www.thehotelastoria.com
Tel.: +7 (812) 313 5757
Fax: +7 (812) 313 5059

**Stoke Park Club**  (UK)
Park Road, Stoke Poges
Buckinghamshire
SL2 4PG
www.stokeparkclub.com
Tel.: +44 (1753) 717 171
Fax: +44 (1753) 717 181

**Knightsbridge**  (UK)
10 Beaufort Gardens
London
SW3 1PT
www.firmdale.com
Tel.: +44 (20) 7584 6300
Fax: +44 (20) 7584 6355

**Threadneedles**  (UK)
5 Threadneedles Street
London
EC2R 8AY
www.theetoncollection.com
Tel.: +44 (20) 7657 8080
Fax: +44 (20) 7657 8100

**Hotel Pulitzer**  (NL)
Prinsengracht 315-331
1016 GZ Amsterdam
www.starwood.com/luxury
Tel.: +31 (20) 523 5235
Fax: +31 (20) 627 6753

**Amigo**  (B)
Rue de l'Amigo 1-3
1000 Brussels
www.hotelamigo.com
Tel.: +32 (2) 547 4747
Fax: +32 (2) 513 5277

**The Regent Schlosshotel Berlin**  (D)
Brahmsstraße 10
14193 Berlin
www.schlosshotelberlin.com
Tel.: +49 (30) 8958 40
Fax: +49 (30) 8958 4800

**Hotel zur Bleiche**  (D)
Bleichestraße 16
03096 Burg/Spreewald
www.hotel-zur-bleiche.de
Tel.: +49 (35603) 620
Fax: +49 (35603) 602 92

**Grand Hotel Heiligendamm**  (D)
18209 Heiligendamm
www.grandhotel-heiligendamm.de
Tel.: +49 (38203) 740 0
Fax: +49 (38203) 740 7474

**Mandarin Oriental**  (D)
Neuturmstraße 1
80331 München
www.mandarinoriental.com
Tel.: +49 (89) 290 980
Fax: +49 (89) 222 539

**La Réserve**  (CH)
301, Route de Lausanne
1293 Genève
www.lareserve.ch
Tel.: +41 (22) 959 5959
Fax: +41 (22) 959 5960

**Palace Luzern**  (CH)
Haldenstraße 10
6002 Luzern
www.palace-luzern.ch
Tel.: +41 (41) 416 1616
Fax: +41 (41) 416 1000

**Hôtel Palafitte**  (CH)
2 Route des Gouttes d'Or
2000 Neuchâtel
www.palafitte.ch
Tel.: +41 (32) 723 0202
Fax: +41 (32) 723 0203

**Hôtel des Trois Couronnes**  (CH)
49, rue d'Italie
1800 Vevey
www.hotel3couronnes.ch
Tel.: +41 (21) 923 3200
Fax: +41 (21) 923 3399

**Hotel Imperial**  (A)
Kärntner Ring 16
1015 Wien
www.starwood.com/luxury
Tel.: +43 (1) 501 100
Fax: +43 (1) 5011 0410

**Plaza Athénée**  (F)
25, Avenue Montaigne
75008 Paris
www.plaza-athenee-paris.com
Tel.: +33 (1) 5367 6665
Fax: +33 (1) 5367 6666

**Château de Massillan**  (F)
Chemin Hauteville
84100 Uchaux
www.chateau-de-massillan.com
Tel.: +33 (490) 406 451
Fax: +33 (490) 406 385

**Villa d'Este**  (I)
Via Regina, 40
22012 Cernobbio
www.villadeste.com
Tel.: +39 (031) 348 1
Fax: +39 (031) 348 873

**Villa San Michele**  (I)
Via Doccia, 4
50014 Firenze
www.villasanmichele.orient-express.com
Tel.: +39 (055) 567 8200
Fax: +39 (055) 567 8250

**Villa Feltrinelli**  (I)
Via Rimembranza 38-40
25084 Gargnano
www.villafeltrinelli.com
Tel.: +39 (0365) 798 000
Fax: +39 (0365) 798 001

**Four Seasons Hotel Milano**  (I)
Via Gesù 8
20121 Milano
www.fourseasons.com/milan
Tel.: +39 (02) 7708 8
Fax: +39 (02) 7708 5000

**Brufani Palace**  (I)
Piazza Italia 12
06100 Perugia
www.sinahotels.com
Tel.: +39 (075) 573 2541
Fax: +39 (075) 572 0210

**Hotel de Russie**  (I)
Via del Babuino 9
00187 Roma
www.hotelderussie.it
Tel.: +39 (06) 3288 81
Fax: +39 (06) 3288 8888

**Bauer Venezia**  (I)
San Marco 1459
30124 Venezia
www.bauervenezia.com
Tel.: +39 (041) 520 7022
Fax: +39 (041) 520 7557

**Danieli**  (I)
Castello 4196
30122 Venezia
www.starwood.com/luxury
Tel.: +39 (041) 522 6480
Fax: +39 (041) 520 0208

**San Clemente Palace**  (I)
Isola di San Clemente, 1
30124 Venezia
www.sanclemente.thi.it
Tel.: +39 (41) 244 5001
Fax: +39 (41) 244 5800

**Choupana Hills Resort & Spa**  (P)
Travessa do Largo da Choupana
9060-348 Funchal-Madeira
www.choupanahills.com
Tel.: +351 (291) 206 020
Fax: +351 (291) 206 021

# Hôtels Internationaux  Internationale Hotels  International Hotels
## Internationale Hotels  Hoteles Internacionales  Alberghi Internazionali

**Palácio Belmonte** (P)
Páteo Dom Fradique 14
1100-624 Lisboa
www.palaciobelmonte.com
Tel.: +351 (21) 881 6600
Fax: +351 (21) 881 6609

**Gran Hotel La Florida** (E)
Carretera de Vallvidrera al Tibidabo 83-93
08035 Barcelona
www.hotellaflorida.com
Tel.: +34 (93) 259 3000
Fax: +34 (93) 259 3001

**Hesperia** (E)
Paseo de la Castellana 57
28046 Madrid
www.hesperia-madrid.com
Tel.: +34 (91) 210 8800
Fax: +34 (91) 210 8899

**Rio Real Golf Hotel** (E)
Urbanización Río Real
29603 Marbella
www.rioreal.com
Tel.: +34 (952) 765 732
Fax: +34 (952) 772 140

**Hotel Alfonso XIII** (E)
San Fernando 2
41004 Sevilla
www.westin.com/hotelalfonso
Tel.: +34 (95) 491 7000
Fax: +34 (95) 491 7099

**Grand Resort Lagonissi** (GR)
40 km Athens-Sounio Ave.
19010 Lagonissi
www.lagonissiresort.gr
Tel.: +30 (22910) 760 00
Fax: +30 (22910) 245 34

**Danai Beach Resort** (GR)
Nikiti
63088 Chalkidiki
www.dbr.gr
Tel.: +30 (23750) 20400
Fax: +30 (23750) 22591

**Belvedere Hotel** (GR)
School of Fine Arts District
84600 Mykonos
www.belvederehotel.com
Tel.: +30 (2289) 0 251 22
Fax: +30 (2289) 0 251 26

**Almyra** (CY)
P.O. Box 60136
8125 Pafos
www.thanoshotels.com
Tel.: +357 (26) 933 091
Fax: +357 (26) 942 818

## Cosmopolitan Hotels

**Hotel St-Paul** (CDN)
355 rue McGill
Montreal, Quebec H2Y 2E8
www.hotelstpaul.com
Tel.: +1 514 380 2222
Fax: +1 514 380 2200

**Hôtel Le Germain** (CDN)
2050 rue Mansfield
Montreal, Quebec H3A 1Y9
www.hotelgermain.com
Tel.: +1 514 849 2050
Fax: +1 514 849 1437

**ARC The Hotel** (CDN)
140 Slater Street
Ottawa, Ontario K1P 5H6
www.arcthehotel.com
Tel.: +1 613 238 2888
Fax: +1 613 238 0053

**Opus Hotel** (CDN)
322 Davie Street
Vancouver, British Columbia V6B 5Z6
www.opushotel.com
Tel.: +1 604 642 6787
Fax: +1 604 642 6780

**Hotel Lucia** (USA)
400 SW Broadway
Portland, Oregon 97205
www.hotellucia.com
Tel.: +1 503 225 1717
Fax: +1 503 225 1919

**Chateau Marmont** (USA)
8221 Sunset Boulevard
West Hollywood, California 90046
www.chateaumarmont.com
Tel.: +1 323 656 1010
Fax: +1 323 655 5311

**Sunset Marquis Hotel and Villas** (USA)
1200 Alta Loma Road
West Hollywood, California 90069
www.sunsetmarquishotel.com
Tel.: +1 310 657 1333
Fax: +1 310 652 5300

**The Ambrose Hotel** (USA)
1255 20th Street
Santa Monica, California 90404
www.ambrosehotel.com
Tel.: +1 310 315 1555
Fax: +1 310 315 1556

**Loft 523** (USA)
523 Gravier Street
New Orleans, Louisiana 70130
www.loft523.com
Tel.: +1 504 200 6523
Fax: +1 504 200 6522

**The Shore Club** (USA)
1901 Collins Avenue
South Beach, Miami, Florida 33139
www.shoreclub.com
Tel.: +1 305 695 3100
Fax: +1 305 695 3299

**The Tides South Beach** (USA)
1220 Ocean Drive
Miami Beach, Florida 33139
www.tidessouthbeach.com
Tel.: +1 305 604 5070
Fax: +1 310 503 3275

**The Bryant Park** (USA)
40 W 40th Street
New York, New York 10018
www.bryantparkhotel.com
Tel.: +1 212 869 0100
Fax: +1 212 869 4446

**Chambers Hotel** (USA)
15 W 56th Street
New York, New York 10019
www.chambersnyc.com
Tel.: +1 212 974 5656
Fax: +1 212 974 5657

**Sixty Thompson** (USA)
60 Thompson Street
New York, New York 10012
www.60thompson.com
Tel.: +1 877 431 0400
Fax: +1 212 431 0200

**The Time** (USA)
224 W 49th Street
New York, New York 10019
www.thetimeny.com
Tel.: +1 212 980 9060
Fax: +1 212 245 2305

**W Times Square** (USA)
1567 Broadway/47th Street
New York, New York 10036
www.whotels.com
Tel.: +1 212 930 7400
Fax: +1 212 930 7500

**The Water & Beach Club** (PR)
2 Tartak Street
Isla Verde, San Juan
Carolina, Puerto Rico 00979
www.waterbeachclubhotel.com
Tel.: +1 787 728 3666
Fax: +1 787 728 3610

# International Hotels  Internationale Hotels  Hôtels Internationaux
## Alberghi Internazionali  Hoteles Internacionales  Internationale Hotels

**Design Suites** (AR)
Marcelo T. de Alvear 1683
Buenos Aires, 1060
www.designsuites.com
Tel.: +54 11 4814 8700
Fax: +54 11 4814 8700

**Hotel Unique** (BR)
Av Brigadeiro Luís Antônio, 4700
Jd. Paulista, São Paulo
CEP 01402-002
www.hotelunique.com.br
Tel.: +55 11 3055 4710
Fax: +55 11 3889 8100

**Hotel Birger Jarl** (S)
Tulegatan 8
10432 Stockholm
www.birgerjarl.se
Tel.: +46 8 674 1800
Fax: +46 8 673 7366

**Nordic Light Hotel** (S)
Vasaplan 7, Box 884
10137 Stockholm
www.nordichotels.se
Tel.: +46 8 5056 3000
Fax: +46 8 5056 3060

**Radisson Blu Royal Hotel** (DK)
Hammerichsgade 1
Copenhagen DK-1611
www.radissonsas.com
Tel.: +45 33 42 60 00
Fax: +45 33 42 61 00

**The Glasshouse** (UK)
2 Greenside Place
Edinburgh EH1 3AA
www.theetoncollection.com
Tel.: +44 131 525 8200
Fax: +44 131 525 8205

**Charlotte Street Hotel** (UK)
15-17 Charlotte Street
London W1T 1RJ
www.charlottestreethotel.com
Tel.: +44 20 7806 2000
Fax: +44 20 7806 2002

**Sherlock Holmes Hotel** (UK)
108 Baker Street
London W1U 6LJ
www.sherlockholmeshotel.com
Tel.: +44 20 7486 6161
Fax: +44 20 7958 5211

**The Lowry Hotel** (UK)
50 Dearmans Place
Chapel Wharf
Manchester M3 5LH
www.thelowryhotel.com
Tel.: +44 161 827 4000
Fax: +44 161 827 4001

**Hotel Brandenburger Hof** (D)
Eislebener Straße 14
10789 Berlin
www.brandenburgerhof.com
Tel.: +49 30 21405 0
Fax: +49 30 21405 100

**Grand Hyatt Berlin** (D)
Marlene-Dietrich-Platz 2
10785 Berlin
www.berlin.grand.hyatt.de
Tel.: +49 30 2553 1234
Fax: +49 30 2553 1235

**The Mandala Hotel** (D)
Potsdamer Straße 3
10785 Berlin
www.madison-berlin.de
Tel.: +49 30 590 05 0000
Fax: +49 30 590 05 0500

**Sofitel Hamburg Alter Wall** (D)
Alles Wall 40
20457 Hamburg
www.sofitel.com
Tel.: +49 40 36 95 00
Fax: +49 40 36 95 01 000

**Cortiina Hotel** (D)
Ledererstraße 8
80331 München
www.cortiina.com
Tel.: +49 89 242 2490
Fax: +49 89 242 249100

**Ramada Plaza Basel** (CH)
Messeplatz 12
4058 Basel
www.ramada-treff.ch
Tel.: +41 61 560 4000
Fax: +41 61 560 5555

**Hôtel Angleterre & Résidence** (CH)
Place du Port 11
1006 Lausanne
www.angleterre-residence.ch
Tel.: +41 21 613 3434
Fax: +41 21 613 3435

**Hotel Josef** (CZ)
Rybna 20
110 00 Prague 1
www.hoteljosef.com
Tel.: +420 2 2170 0111
Fax: +420 2 2170 0999

**Le Dokhan's** (F)
117, rue Lauriston
75116 Paris
www.radissonblu.com
Tel.: +33 1 5365 6699
Fax: +33 1 5365 6688

**Hôtel de la Trémoille** (F)
14, rue de la Trémoille
75008 Paris
www.hotel-tremoille.com
Tel.: +33 1 5652 1400
Fax: +33 1 4070 0108

**J.K. Place** (I)
Piazza Santa Maria Novella, 7
50123 Florence
www.jkplace.com
Tel.: +39 055 264 5181
Fax: +39 055 265 8387

**Enterprise Hotel** (I)
Corso Sempione, 91
20154 Milan
www.enterprisehotel.com
Tel.: +39 02 3181 81
Fax: +39 02 3181 8811

**Aleph** (I)
Via di San Basilio, 15
00187 Rome
www.aleph.boscolohotels.com
Tel.: +39 06 422 901
Fax: +39 06 422 90000

**Hotel Arts Barcelona** (E)
Carrer de la Marina, 19-21
08005 Barcelona
www.ritzcarlton.com/hotels/barcelona
Tel.: +34 93 221 1000
Fax: +34 93 221 1070

**Hotel Banys Orientals** (E)
C. Argenteria, 37
08003 Barcelona
www.hotelbanysorientals.com
Tel.: +34 93 268 8460
Fax: +34 93 268 8461

**Gran Hotel Domine** (E)
Alameda de Mazarredo, 61
48009 Bilbao
www.granhoteldominebilbao.com
Tel.: +34 944 253 300
Fax: +34 944 253 301

**Solar Do Castelo** (P)
Rua das Cozinhas, 2 (ao Castelo)
1100-181 Lisbon
www.heritage.pt/en/solardocastelo.htm
Tel.: +351 218 806 050
Fax: +351 218 870 907

# Hôtels Internationaux  Internationale Hotels  International Hotels
## Internationale Hotels  Hoteles Internacionales  Alberghi Internazionali

**Ten Bompas** (ZA)
10 Bompas Road
Dunkeld West, Sandton 2146
Gauteng, Johannesburg
www.tenbompas.com
Tel.: +27 11 341 0282
Fax: +27 11 341 0281

**Saxon** (ZA)
36 Saxon Road, Sandhurst
Johannesburg
www.thesaxon.com
Tel.: +27 11 292 6000
Fax: +27 11 292 6001

**Kensington Place** (ZA)
38 Kensington Crescent, Higgovale
Cape Town, 8001
www.kensingtonplace.co.za
Tel.: +27 21 424 4744
Fax: +27 21 424 1810

**The Park Bangalore** (IND)
14/7 Mahatma Gandhi Road
Bangalore – 560 042
www.theparkhotels.com
Tel.: +91 80 2559 4666
Fax: +91 80 2559 4667

**The Strand** (MM)
92 Strand Road
Yangon
www.ghmhotels.com
Tel.: +95 1 243 377
Fax: +95 1 243 393

**The Fullerton** (SGP)
1 Fullerton Square
Singapore 049178
www.fullertonhotel.com
Tel.: +65 6733 8388
Fax: +65 6735 8388

**Hotel Lindrum** (AUS)
26 Flinders Street
Melbourne, Victoria 3000
www.hotellindrum.com.au
Tel.: +61 3 9668 1111
Fax: +61 3 9668 1199

**Establishment** (AUS)
5 Bridge Lane
Sydney, New South Wales 2000
www.luxehotels.com/hotels/establishment
Tel.: +61 2 9240 3100
Fax: +61 2 9240 3101

## Cool Hotels

**Side Hotel** (D)
Drehbahn 49
20354 Hamburg
Tel.: +49 40 30 99 90
Fax: +49 40 30 99 93

**Wasserturm** (D)
Kaygasse 2
50676 Köln
Tel.: +49 221 20 080
Fax: +49 221 20 08888

**Gastwerk Hotel** (D)
Beim Alten Gaswerk 3
Daimlerstraße
22761 Hamburg
Tel.: +49 40 890 62-0
Fax: +49 40 890 62-20

**Blakes Amsterdam** (NL)
Keizersgracht 384
Amsterdam 1016 GB
Tel.: +31 20 530 20 10
Fax: +31 20 530 20 30

**The Lady's First Hotel** (CH)
Mainaustraße 24
8008 Zürich
Tel.: +41(0) 44 380 80 10
Fax: +41(0) 44 380 80 20

**Widder Hotel** (CH)
Rennweg 7
8001 Zürich
Tel.: +41 (0)44 224 2526
Fax: +41 (0)44 224 2424

**Das Triest** (A)
Wiedner Hauptstraße 12
1040 Wien
Tel.: +43 1 589 18-0
Fax: +43 1 589 18-18

**Saint Martin's Lane** (UK)
45 Saint Martins Lane
London
WC2N 4HX
Tel.: +44 207 300 5500
Fax: +44 207 300 5501

**One Aldwych** (UK)
1 Aldwych
London
WC2B 4BZ
Tel.: +44 207 300 1000
Fax: +44 207 300 1001

**The Hempel** (UK)
31-35 Craven Hill Gardens
London
W2 3EA
Tel.: +44 20 7298 9000
Fax: +44 20 7402 4666

**Hotel Square** (F)
3 Rue de Boulainvilliers
75016 Paris
Tel: +33 14 414 9190
Fax: +33 14 414 9199

**Hotel Montalembert** (F)
3 Rue de Montalembert
75007 Paris
Tel.: +33 14 549 6868
Fax: +33 14 549 6949

**Gallery Hotel Art** (I)
Vicolo Dell'Oro 5
50123 Florence
Tel.: +39 055 272 63
Fax: +39 055 268 557

**Hotel Diplomatic** (E)
Pau Claris, 122
08009 Barcelona
Tel.: +34 93 272 3810
Fax: +34 93 272 3811

**Hotel Portixol** (E)
Sirena, 27
070006 Palma de Mallorca
Tel.: +34 971 271 800
Fax: +34 971 275 025

**Ace Hotel** (USA)
2423 1st Avenue
Seattle, WA 98121
Tel.: +1 206 448 4721
Fax: +1 206 374 0745

**Hudson Rocks** (USA)
356 West 58th Street
New York, NY 10019
Tel.: +1 212 554 6000
Fax: +1 212 554 6001

**W NY Union Square** (USA)
201 Park Avenue South
New York, NY 10003
Tel.: +1 212 253 9119
Fax: +1 212 253 9229

**W Los Angeles** (USA)
930 Hilgard Avenue
Los Angeles, CA 90024
Tel.: +1 310 208 8765
Fax: +1 310 824 0355

**Maison 140** (USA)
140 South Lasky Drive
Beverly Hills, CA 90212
Tel.: +1 310 281 4000
Fax: +1 310 281 4001

**The Hotel** (USA)
801 Collins Avenue
Miami Beach, FL 33139
Tel.: +1 305 531 2222
Fax: +1 305 531 3222

# International Hotels  Internationale Hotels  Hôtels Internationaux
## Alberghi Internazionali  Hoteles Internacionales  Internationale Hotels

**Orbit In**  (USA)
562 W. Arenas
Palm Springs, CA 92262

Tel.: +1 760 323 3585
Fax: +1 760 323 3599

**Kirketon**  (AUS)
229 Darlinghurst Rd.
Darlinghurst NSW 2010
Sydney

Tel.: +61 2 9332 2211
Fax: +61 2 9332 2499

**The Prince**  (AUS)
2 Acland Street, St. Kilda
Melbourne 3182

Tel.: +61 3 95 36 1111
Fax: +61 3 95 36 1100

**Devi Gahr Palace**  (IND)
PO Box no. 144
Udaipur 313001
Rajasthan

Tel.: +91 2953 2 89 211
Fax: +91 2953 2 89 357

**The Manor**  (IND)
77 Friends
Colony [West]
New Delhi 110065

Tel.: +91 11 2 692 5151
Fax: +91 11 2 692 2299

**Le Méridien**  (PF)
PO Box 190
Motu Tape, Bora Bora
French Polynesia

Tel.: +689 60 51 51
Fax: +689 60 51 52

## Country Hotels

**Babington House**  (UK)
Babington
NR Frome
Somerset BA11 3RW

Tel.: +44 1373 812 266
Fax: +44 1373 812 112

**L'Oustau de Baumaniére**  (F)
Val d'Enfer
13520 Les Baux de Provence

Tel.: +33 490 54 3307
Fax: +33 490 54 4046

**Tenuta San Vito**  (I)
Via San Vito 59
50056 Montelupo Fiorentino
Florence

Tel.: +39 0571 514 11
Fax: +39 0571 514 05

**Torre di Bellosguardo**  (I)
Via Roti Michelozzi 2
50124 Florence

Tel.: +39 055 229 8145
Fax: +39 055 229 008

**La Saracina**  (I)
S.S. 146 Km 29.7
53026 Pienza
Siena

Tel.: +39 0578 748 022
Fax: +39 0578 748 018

**Quinta Do Juncal**  (P)
Serra D'el Rei
2525-801 Peniche
Portugal

Tel.: +351 262 905 030
Fax: +351 262 905 031

**Lindos Huéspedes**  (E)
Carretera de Pals
Torroella de Montgri
Girona

Tel./Fax:
+34 972 66 82 03

**La Fuente de la Higuera**  (E)
Partido de los Frontones
29400 Ronda
Malaga

Tel.: +34 952 1143 55
Fax: +34 952 656 09

**Ca's Xorc**  (E)
Carretera de Deia, Km 56,1
07100 Soller
Mallorca

Tel.: +34 971 638 280
Fax: +34 971 632 949

**Hospedería Parque
de Monfragüe**  (E)
Carretera Plasencia-Trujillo,
Km 37
10694 Torrejon el Rubio
Caceres

Tel.: +34 927 455 78
Fax: +34 927 455 280

**Caravanserai**  (MA)
264 Ouled Ben Rahmoune
40000 Marrakesh

Tel.: +212 524 30 03 02
Fax: +212 524 30 02 62

**Hotel Les Deux Tours**  (MA)
Douar Abiad
25/26/27
13P513 Marrakesh Principale

Tel.: +212 524 32 95 25
Fax: +212 524 32 95 23

**The Mill House Inn**  (USA)
31 North Main Street
East Hampton, NY 11937

Tel./Fax:
+1 631 324 9766

**The Inn at Saw Mill Farm**  (USA)
7, Crosstown Trail
West Dover, VT 05356

Tel.: +1 800 493 1133
Fax: +1 800 493 1130

**Acqua Hotel**  (USA)
555 Redwood Highway
Mill Valley, CA 94941

Tel.: +1 415 380 0400
Fax: +1 415 380 9696

**Lake Placid Lodge**  (USA)
144 Lodge Way
Lake Placid, NY 12946

Tel.: +1 518 523 2700
Fax: +1 518 523 1124

**Pira Lodge**  (RA)
Pasaje de "El Boqueron"
Mercedes
Provincia de Corrientes

Tel.: +54 1143 3197 10
Fax: +54 3773 4203 99

**La Pascuala Delta Lodge**  (RA)
Delta del Rio Parana
Argentina

Tel.: +54 11 4728
      1253/1395
Fax: +54 11 4728
      1475/2070

**Bali Spirit Hotel and Spa**  (RI)
189 Nyuh Kuning
Ubud
Bali 80571

Tel.: +62 361 974 013
Fax: +62 361 974 012

# Internationale Abkürzungen International Trade Abbreviations
## Abréviations Commerciales

| | |
|---|---|
| a.a.r. | against all risks, Versicherung gegen alle Gefahren |
| a/c | a conto, account, Rechnung |
| A/C | account current, Kontokorrent |
| A/T | American terms (insurance) |
| acct. | account, Rechnung |
| Av. | average, Havarie, Schaden |
| B.L., B/L | Bill of lading, Schiffsfrachtbrief |
| c.a.d. (c/d) | cash against documents, Zahlung gegen Dokumente |
| c.a.f. | cost, assurance, freight included, Kosten, Versicherung, Fracht |
| cf., c.f., c&f | cost and freight, Kosten und Fracht |
| c.i., c&i | cost and insurance, Einstandspreis und Versicherung |
| C/I | certificate of insurance, Versicherungspolice |
| C.I.A. | cash in advance, Zahlung im Voraus |
| c.i.f. | cost, insurance, freight included, Kosten, Versicherungsprämie, Fracht eingeschlossen |
| c.i.f. & c. | cost, insurance, freight & commission, c.i.f. + Kommission |
| c.i.f.c. & i. | cost, insurance, freight, commission & interest, c.i.f.c. + Bankzinsen |
| c.o.d., cod | cash collect on delivery, Zahlung bei Auslieferung oder Empfang |
| c.o.s. | cash on shipment, Zahlung bei Verschiffung |
| C.W.O. | cash with order, Zahlung mit Anweisung |
| D.A., D/A | documents against acceptance, Dokumente gegen Akzeptierung einer Tratte |
| D.A.D. | documents against disposition, Dokumente gegen Verfügung (über Ladung) |
| d.f. | dead freight, Fautfracht für nicht genutzten Laderaum |
| D/N | debit note, Lastschrift |
| D.O. (D/o) | delivery order, Auslieferungsanweisung |
| d/p | documents against payment, Dokumente gegen Zahlung |
| D/W | dock warrant, Ladeplatz-Berechtigung |
| E.c. | English conditions (insurance), Englische Bedingungen (Versicherung) |
| E.O.M. | end of month, zum Monatsende |
| F | first class, Erster Klasse |
| f.a.a., faa | free of all average, frei von jedem Schaden |
| f.a.s. | free alongside ship, frei Längsseite Schiff |
| f.b.h. | free on board at harbor, frei an Bord im Hafen |
| F & D | freight and demurrage, Fracht und Liegegeld |
| F.F.A. | free from alongside, frei von Längsseite her |
| Fgt. (frt.) | freight, Fracht |
| f.i.o. | free in and out, frei Ein- und Ausladen und Löschen |
| f.o.a. | free on aircraft, frei an Bord des Flugzeugs |
| f.o.b., fob | free on board, frei an Bord |
| f.o.c. | free on charge, frei an Belastung, Forderung |
| f.o.d. | free of damage, frei von Schaden |
| f.o.q. | free on quay, frei auf Kai |
| f.o.r. | free on rail, frei Bahnhof oder auf Güterwagen |
| FOR | free on road, frei bis Straße |
| f.o.s. | free on ship, frei ins Schiff |
| f.o.t. | free on truck, frei auf Güterwagen, LKW oder Bahnhof |
| f.o.w. | free on wagon, frei auf Güterwagen |
| f.p.a. | free of particular average, frei von Beschädigung, außer Strandungsfall |
| frt. pp. | freight prepaid, Fracht bezahlt |
| g.a., G/A | general average, große Havarie, großer Schaden |
| I.B. | in bond, unverzollte Ware unter Zollverschluss |
| int. | interests, Bankzinsen |
| i.p.a. | including particular average, Beschädigung von Waren eingeschlossen |
| i.t. | immediate transport, sofortiger, unmittelbarer Transport |
| L/C | letter of credit, Kreditbrief, Akkreditiv |
| L.&D. | loss and damage, Verlust und Schaden |
| M.D. | month's date, Monatsdatum |
| M.I.P | marine insurance policy, See-Versicherungspolice |
| M/P | months after payment, Zahlung nächsten Monat |
| M/R | mate's receipt, Quittung des Landungsoffiziers über Empfang der Ware an Bord |
| N | night-flight, Nachtflug |
| N/t | new terms, neue Vertragsbedingungen |
| n.wt. | net weight, Nettogewicht |
| O.P. | open floating policy (insurance), offene oder laufende Police |
| O.R.D. | owner's risk of damage, Eigners Gefahr bei Schaden |
| O/T | old terms, alte Vertragsbedingungen |
| P/a | particular average, besondere Beschädigung von Waren durch Transportunfälle |
| pd. | paid, Bezahlung |
| P.L. | partial loss, Teilschaden |
| P/N | promissory note, Eigen-, Solawechsel |
| P.O.D. | pay on delivery, Zahlung bei Lieferung, Zustellung |
| ppd. | prepaid, Vorauszahlung |
| ppt. | promptly, sofort liefer- und zahlbar |
| rect. (rept.) | receipt, Eingang der Ware, Empfang |
| R.I. | reinsurance, Rückversicherung |
| RP | reply paid, Rückzahlung |
| S.&F.A. | shipping and forwarding agent, Schiffsspediteur |
| s.g. (sp.gr.) | specific gravity, spezifisches Gewicht, Gewichte |
| S/N | shipping note, Schiffszettel |
| T/A | trade acceptance, Handelsakzept |
| t.l.o., T.L.O. | total loss only, Totalverlust |
| t.q. | trade quality, Handelssorte, Handelsqualität |
| tr. | tare, Tara |
| uc. | usual conditions, gewöhnliche Bedingungen |
| u.t. | usual terms, übliche Vertragsbedingungen |
| U/w | underwriter, Versicherer |
| W.B. | way bill, Versandavis, Bordero, Frachtkarte, Frachtbrief |
| w.g. | weight guaranteed, garantiertes Gewicht |
| w/m, W/M | weight or measurement, Maß oder Gewicht |
| wpa | with particular average, mit Teilschaden, d. h. jede Beschädigung ist vom Versicherer zu ersetzen |
| W.R. | war risk, Kriegsrisiko |
| W/R | warehouse receipt, Lagerhausbescheinigung |
| wt | weight, Gewicht |
| W/W | warehouse warrant, Lagerhausberechtigung |

*without guarantee

# Management Vocabulary  Management-Vokabular
# Vocabulaire Commercial

| English | French | German |
|---|---|---|
| **account** | compte | Konto |
| appropriation account | comte d'affectation | Rückstellungskonto |
| consolidated accounts | bilan consolidé | konsolidierte Bilanz, Konzernbilanz |
| current account | compte courant | Kontokorrent |
| deposit account | compte de depôt | Depositenkonto |
| profit and loss account | compte de pertes ct profits | Gewinn- und Verlustrechnung |
| statement of account | état de compte, relevé de compte | Kontoauszug |
| accountant | comptable | Rechnungsprüfer, Wirtschaftsprüfer |
| actual | prix courant | Tagespreis |
| actuary | actuaire | Aktuar |
| advertising | publicité | Werbung |
| after-hour-dealings | opérations hors ouverture | Nachbörse |
| agreement | accord | Abkommen, Vertrag |
| allotment letter | lettre d'attribution | Zuteilungsmitteilung |
| amortisation, redemption | amortissement | Tilgung, Amortisation |
| annuity | annuité | Jahresrente |
| life annuity | rente viagère | Leibrente |
| application form | formulaire de souscription | Bezugsformular |
| application money | versement de souscription | Bezugsgeld |
| appreciation | appréciation, plus-value | Wertsteigerung |
| arbitrage | arbitrage | Arbitrage |
| assets | actif | Aktiva, Vermögenswerte |
| current assets | actif circulant, actif réalisable | Umlaufvermögen |
| fixed assets | capital fixe, immobilisations | Anlagevermögen |
| intangible assets | valeurs immatérielles | immaterielle Anlagewerte |
| liquid assets | capital liquide, valeurs réalisables, disponilibités | flüssige Anlagen, flüssige Mittel |
| net assets | valeurs nettes | Reinvermögen |
| trading assets | valeurs d'exploitation | Handelsvermögen |
| associate, partner | associé | Teilhaber, Partner |
| atomic energy | énergie atomique | Kernenergie |
| authorized depositaries | dépositaires autorisés | autorisierte Hinterlegungsstellen |
| automation | automation | Automatisierung |
| averaging | moyennes | Ausgleichskäufe oder -verkäufe |
| **backwardation** | déport | Kursabschlag |
| balance | balance | Saldo |
| invisible trade balance | balance commerciale invisible | Dienstleistungsbilanz |
| trade balance | balance commerciale | Leistungsbilanz |
| visible trade balance | balance commerciale visible | Handelsbilanz, Warenhandelsbilanz |
| balance of payments | balance des paiements | Zahlungsbilanz |
| balance sheet | bilan | Bilanz |
| bank (joint stock) | banque (sous forme de société par actions) | Aktienbank |
| central bank | banque centrale | Zentralbank |
| clearing bank | banque de clearing | Clearingbank, Verrechnungsbank |
| | banque de compensation | |
| commercial bank | banque commerciale | Handelsbank |
| merchant bank | banque d'affaires | Remboursbank |
| savings bank | caisse d'épargne | Sparkasse |
| bank rate | taux officiel (d'escompte) | Diskontsatz |
| bankruptcy | faillite | Konkurs, Bankrott |
| bargain | transaction | Abschluss, Geschäft |
| bear | baissier | Baissier, Baissespekulant |
| bear market | marché orienté à la baisse | Baissemarkt |
| bid | offre | Angebot |
| takeover bid | offre publique d'achat (OPA) | Übernahmeangebot |
| bill of lading | connaissement | Konnossement, Seefrachtbrief |
| blue chips | effets solides | Spitzenwerte |
| board of directors | conseil d'administration | Vorstand |
| bond | obligation | Obligation, Schuldverschreibung |
| bonded warehouse | entrepôt hors douane | Zollniederlage, Zollspeicher |
| boom | boom | Hausse, Hochkonjunktur |
| broker | courtier, agent de change | Makler |
| brokerage | courtage | Maklergeschäft |
| budget | budget | Budget, Haushalt, Voranschlag |
| budgetary control | contrôle budgetaire | Etatkontrolle |
| bull | haussier | Haussier, Haussespekulant |
| business | affaires | Geschäft |
| buying-in | rachat | Eindeckung |
| **call option** | prime à la hausse | Kaufoption, Bezugsoption |
| calls | appels de fonds | Zahlungsaufforderung |
| authorized capital | capital autorisé | genehmigtes Kapital |
| issued capital | capital émis | ausgegebenes Kapital |
| ordinary capital | actions ordinaires | Stammaktienkapital |
| working capital | capital d'exploitation, capital dc roulement | Betriebskapital |
| capital distribution | distribution de capital | Kapitalausschüttung |
| capital gains tax | impôt sur la plus-value du capital | Kapitalzuwachssteuer |
| capital goods | biens d'équipement | Investitionsgüter |
| capital intensive | capitalistique | Kapitalintensive |
| capital issue | émission d'actions | Effektenemission |
| capital reduction | réduction de capital | Kapitalherabsetzung |
| capital reserves | réserves de capital | Kapitalreserven |
| capital spending | investissements | Kapitalaufwand |
| cargo handling | manutention | Güterumschlag |
| cash bonus | prime en espèces | Barprämie |
| cash flow | circulation monétaire | Geldumlauf |
| discounted cash flow | cash flow actualisé | diskontierter Geldumlauf |
| cash settlement | règlement en espèces | Barbegleichung |
| cash transaction | transaction au comptant | Bartransaktion |
| certificate | certificat | Zertifikat, Aktienschein |
| certification | certification | Überweisungsausweis |
| chairman | président | Vorsitzender |
| charter | charte | Charter |
| cheap | bon marché | billig |
| cheap money | agent facile | billiges Geld |
| c.i.f. | c.a.f. | c.i.f. |
| (cost, insurance, freight) | (coût, assurance, frêt) | (Kosten, Versicherung, Fracht) |
| claim | réclamation | Anspruch |
| closing prices | cours de clôture | Schlussnotierung |
| c.o.d. (cash on delivery) | livraison contre remboursement | zahlbar bei Lieferung |
| collateral | collatéral | Deckung, Sicherheit |
| commission | commission | Provision |
| commodity | produit, denrée, matière | Artikel, Ware, Rohstoff |
| common stocks/shares | actions ordinaires | Stammaktie |
| company | société | Gesellschaft |
| associate company | société affiliée, société apparentée | nahestehende Gesellschaft |
| holding company | société holding | Holdinggesellschaft |
| limited liability company | société à responsabilité limitée, société anonyme | Gesellschaft mit beschränkter Haftung |
| parent company | société-mère | Mutter-, Stammgesellschaft |
| partnership company | société en commandite | Partnergesellschaft |
| subsidiary company | filiale | Tochtergesellschaft |
| competition | concurrence | Wettbewerb |
| component | composant | Bestandteil |
| computer | ordinateur | Computer |
| consideration | valeur d'échange | Tauschwert |
| consols | fonds consolidés | Konsols, konsolidierte Staatspapiere |
| consultant | conseiller | Berater |
| consumer | consommateur | Verbraucher |
| consumer goods | biens de consommation | Verbrauchsgüter |
| containerization | conteneurisation | Umstellung auf Container |
| contango | report | Report |
| contingent liability | obligation éventuelle | Eventualverbindlichkeit |
| contract | contrat | Vertrag, Kontrakt |
| control system | système de contrôle | Kontrollsystem |
| conveyancing | cession des biens, transfert | Eigentumsübertragung |
| co-operative society | société en co-opérative | (Konsum-) Genossenschaft |
| cost | coût | Kosten |
| factor cost | coût par facteur de production | Faktorkosten |
| selling costs | frais de vente | Verkaufskosten |
| cost of living | coût de la vie | Lebenshaltungskosten |
| coupon | coupon | Kupon |
| credit | crédit | Kredit, Gutschrift |
| credit balance | solde créditeur | Kreditsaldo |
| credit squeeze | reserrement du crédit, bloquage | Kreditbeschränkung, Kreditrestriktion |
| creditor | créancier | Gläubiger |
| critical path analysis | analyse du chemin critique | kritische Methodenanalyse |
| currency | monnaie | Währung |
| convertible currency | monnaie convertible | konvertible Währung |
| hard currency | monnaie forte | harte Währung |
| soft currency | monnaie faible | weiche Währung |
| current yield | revenu courant | laufende Rendite |
| customs duty | droit de douane | Zoll |

# Management-Vokabular  Management Vocabulary
## Vocabulaire Commercial

| English | French | German |
|---|---|---|
| **data processing** | informatique | Datenverarbeitung |
| deal | transaction | Geschäft |
| dealer | fournisseur | Händler |
| dear money | argent chèr | teures Geld |
| debenture | obligation | Schuldverschreibung |
| debt | dette | Schuld |
|   national debt | dette nationale | Staatsschuld |
| debtor | débiteur | Schuldner |
| deed of transfer | acte de cession | Übertragungsurkunde |
| defaulter | failli (dette privée), concussionnaire (dette publique) | Schuldner |
| deficit financing | déficit-financing | Defizitfinancing, Defizitwirtschaft |
| deflation | déflation | Deflation |
| delivery | livraison | Lieferung |
|   delivery date | date de livraison | Lieferungstermin |
| demand | demande | Nachfrage, Bedarf |
| deposit | dépôt | Depot, Einlage, Einschluss |
| depression, slump | baisse (des cours), malaise, crise, récession (affaires économiques) | Depression, Baisse, Flaute |
| devaluation | dévaluation | Abwertung |
| developing country | pays en voie de développement | Entwicklungsland |
| development | développement | Entwicklung |
| difference | différence | Differenz |
| diminishing returns | rendement décroissant | schrumpfende Erträge |
| director | administrateur | Vorstandsmitglied |
|   managing director | directeur général | Generaldirektor |
| discount, rebate | escompte | Diskont, Rabatt |
| discounted cash flow | circulation monétaire | diskontierter Geldumlauf |
| diversification | diversification | Streuung, Risikostreuung (Anlagen) |
| dividend counterfoil | talon de dividende | Dividendenbogen |
| dividend cover | couverture de dividende | Dividendendeckung |
| dividend/interest warrant | ordonnance de paiement de dividende/des intérêts | Zinsenauszahlungsschein |
| dollar area | zone dollar | Dollargebiet |
| dollar premium | prime en dollars | Dollarprämie |
| dollar stocks | valeurs en dollars | Dollarwertpapiere |
| double option | option double | Doppelprämiengeschäft |
| double-taxation relief | dégrèvement fiscal pour double imposition | Doppelbesteuerungsnachlass |
| drawing board | planche à dessin | Reißbrett |
| drawings | tirage des obligations | Auslösung von Obligationen |
| dumping | dumping | Dumping, Schleuderausfuhr |
| durables | biens d'équipement | langlebige Verbrauchsgüter |
| duty | taxe, douane | Zoll |
|   customs duty | droit de douane | Einfuhrzoll |
|   estate/death duty | droit de succession | Erbschaftssteuer, Nachlasssteuer |
|   stamp duty | droit de timbre | Stempelsteuer |
| **earnings** | bénéfice | Ertrag |
| economics | science économique | Volkswirtschaft |
| economy | économie | Wirtschaft, Ökonomie |
|   economy of scale | économie de marché à grande échelle, économie de masse | Kostenminderung durch große Serien |
| EEC (European Economic Community) | CEE (Communauté Économique Européenne) | EWG (Europäische Wirtschaftsgemeinschaft) |
| EFTA (European Free Trade Association) | AELE (Association Européenne de Libre Échange) | EFTA (Europäische Freihandelszone) |
| elasticity | élasticité | Elastizität |
| embargo | embargo | Sperre, Sperrfrist |
| embassy | ambassade | Botschaft |
| employee | employé | Angestellter, Arbeitnehmer |
| engineer | ingénieur | Ingenieur |
| entrepot | entrepôt | Niederlage, Warenlage |
| equity | actions | Aktien, Aktienkapital, Kapitalanteil |
| estate duty | droit de succession | Erbschaftssteuer, Nachlasssteuer |
| estimate | évaluation | Schätzung, Voranschlag |
| excess shares | excédent de valeurs | überschüssige Wertpapiere |
| exchange | bourse, bourse de change | Börse, Markt |
|   foreign exchange | change | Devisen |
|   exchange control | contrôle des changes | Devisenkontrolle |
|   exchange rate | taux de change | Devisenkurs, Wechselkurs |
|   floating exchange rate | taux de change flottant | gleitender Wechselkurs |
| excise | impôt indirect | Verbrauchsteuer |
| executive | exécutif, dirigeant d'entreprise cadre superiéur | leitender Angestellter |
| export | exportation | Ausfuhr, Export |
|   invisible export | exportation invisible | unsichtbarer Export |
|   visible export | exportation visible | Warenexport |
| **factor cost** | coût des facteurs | Faktorkosten |
| factoring | factoring | Faktoring, Debitorenverkauf |
| factory | usine | Fabrik, Werk |
| final dividend | solde de dividende | Abschlussdividende |
| finance | finances | Finanzen |
| financial year, fiscal year | exercice | Finanzjahr, Geschäftsjahr, Haushaltsjahr |
| firm | société | Firma |
| fiscal | fiscal | fiskalisch |
| fixed charges | frais fixes | feste Spesen |
| flat yield | revenu courant | laufender Ertrag |
| f.o.b. (free on board) | fob (franco à bord) | fob |
| forecast | prévisions | Voraussage |
| foreign investment | investissements étrangers | Auslandsinvestition |
| foreman | contremaître | Vorarbeiter |
| free market | marché libre | freier Markt |
| free trade | libre échange | Freihandel |
| freight | frêt | Fracht |
| fringe benefits | avantages sociaux | Nebenleistungen |
| fund | fonds | Fonds |
| future tax reserve | réserve pour impôts futurs | Steuerreserve für die Zukunft |
| **GDP (gross domestic product)** | Produit Intérieur Brut | Bruttosozialprodukt |
| gilt-edged (securities) | valeurs de premier ordre | mündelsichere Wertpapiere |
| gnome | gnome | Zwerg |
| GNP (gross national product) | PNB (Produit National Brut) | Bruttosozialprodukt |
| gold standard | étalon or | Goldstandard |
| goodwill | droit à la clientèle | Goodwill, Firmenwert |
| gross | brut | brutto |
| growth rate | taux de croissance | Wachstumsrate |
| **hire purchase** | vente à tempérament | Abzahlungsgeschäft |
| hoarding | thésaurisation | hamstern, horten |
| **import** | importation | Import, Einfuhr |
|   import licence | licence d'importation | Einfuhrlizenz |
|   import quota | contingent d'importation | Einfuhrquote, Importquote |
| income | revenu | Einkommen |
|   national income | revenu national | Nationaleinkommen |
|   uncarned income | rente(s) | Einkünfte aus Kapitalbesitz |
|   income tax | impôt sur le revenu | Einkommenssteuer |
| indemnity | indemnité | Entschädigung, Haftpflicht, Garantieversprechung |
| industrial relations | relations industrielles | Beziehungen zwischen Arbeitgeber und Arbeitnehmer |
| input-output analysis | analyse input-output | Input-Output-Analyse |
| installation | équipment, implantation | Einrichtung, Installation |
| instalment | acompte | Rate |
| insurance | assurance | Versicherung |
| intangible assets | valeurs immatérielles | immaterielle Werte |
| interim dividend | dividende intérimaire | Zwischendividende |
| interest (money) | intérêt | Zinsen |
|   (share in) | participation (aux bénéfices) | Anteil |
| majority interest | majorité | Mehrheitsanteil |
| minority | participation minoritaire | Minderheitsanteil |
| interest rate | taux d'intérêt | Zinsfuß |
| inventory | stock | Inventar, Bestand |
| investment (portfolio) | placement | Anlage |
|   (industrial) | investissement | Einsetzung, Investition |
|   foreign investment | investissement étranger | Auslandsinvestition |
|   investment trust | fonds de placement de capitaux, société d'investissement | Investment-Trust, Fonds |
| invoice | facture | Faktura |
| all caps | doit | Schuldschein |
| irredeemables | obligations non remboursables | unkündbare Wertpapiere |
| issue | émission | Emission, Ausgabe |
|   capital issue | émission d'actions | Effektenemission |
|   fiduciary issue | émission fiduciaire | ungedeckte Notenausgabe |
|   new issue | nouvelle émission | Neuausgabe, Neuemission |
|   night issue | émission avec droit de souscription | Ausgabe mit Bezugsrecht |

# Management Vocabulary   Management-Vokabular
## Vocabulaire Commercial

| English | French | German |
|---|---|---|
| scrip capitalization issue | émission d'actions gratuites | Ausgabe mit Bezugsrecht |
| issued capital | capital émis | ausgegebenes Kapital |
| issuing house | maison de placements | Emissionsbank |
| **jobbers** | courtiers intermédiares | Zwischenmakler |
| jobber's spread | marge de l'intermédiaire | Preisspanne des Zwischenmaklers |
| jobbing in and out | spéculation à court terme | kurzfristige Spekulationsgeschäfte |
| **labour-intensive** | à forte intensité de main d'œuvre | arbeitsintensiv |
| lease | bail | Pacht |
| liability | obligation, engagement | Verbindlichkeit |
|   current liability | passif exigible à court terme | laufende Verbindlichkeit |
|   deferred liability | passif à long terme | Rückstellung, rückgestellte Verbindlichkeit |
|   external liability | financement externe | äußere Verbindlichkeit |
| lighterage | chalandage | Leichtergeld, Schutengeld |
| limited liability company | société à responsabilité limitée | GmbH (Gesellschaft mit beschränkter Haftung) |
| limited market | marché étroit | enger Markt |
| liquid | liquide | flüssig, liquid |
| liquidation | liquidation | Liquidation |
| liquidity | liquidités | Liquidität |
| load-factor | taux de charge, indice de charge | Ladefaktor |
| long-term | à long terme | langfristig |
| longs | titres à long terme | langfristige Wertpapiere |
| losses | pertes | Verluste |
| loss-leader | ventes à pertes | Lockartikel |
| low coupon | coupon bas | niedrigverzinster Kupon |
| **machine tool** | machine-outil | Werkzeugmaschine |
| maintenance | entretien | Wartung, Instandhaltung |
| majority-interest | majorité | Mehrheitsbeteiligung |
| make-up prices | prix fixés par la bourse | vom Börsenrat festgesetzte Preise |
| management | gestion | Geschäftsleitung |
| management accountancy | comptabilité de gestion | Management-Rechnungswesen |
| manager | directeur | Manager, Geschäftsleiter |
|   general manager | directeur général | Hauptgeschäftsführer |
| managing director | directeur général | Generaldirektor |
| manufactoring | fabrication | Herstellung |
| margin | marge | Spanne |
|   profit margin | marge bénéficiaire | Gewinnspanne |
| marginal value | valeur marginale | Grenzwert |
| market, business | marché, affaires | Markt |
|   to market | vendre | vermarkten, absetzen |
|   black market | marché noir | schwarzer Markt |
|   forward market | marché à terme | Terminmarkt |
|   rigging the market | provoquer à la bourse une hausse (baisse) artificielle | Marktbeeinflussung, Kursreiberei |
|   spot market | marché au comptant | Kassamarkt |
|   market price | prix de marché | Kurs |
|   at market price | aux prix du marché | zu Marktpreisen |
|   market research | recherche des marchés | Marktforschung |
|   market share | part du marché | Marktanteil |
|   market trend | tendance du marché | Tendenz |
|   market valuation | évaluation basée sur le prix du marché | Marktbewegung |
| marketable security | valeur négociable | marktfähiges Wertpapier |
| marketing | marketing | Vermarktung |
| mass production | production de masse, fabrication en grand série | Massenproduktion |
| materials handling | manutention | Materialförderung |
| maturity | échéance (date of) | Fälligkeit |
| mediums | à moyen terme | mittelfristig |
| medium term | valeurs à moyen terme (5-15 ans) | mittelfristige Wertpapiere (5-15 Jahre) |
| merger | fusion | Fusion, Zusammenschluss |
| middleman | intermédiaire | Mittelsmann, Zwischenhändler |
| minority | participation minoritaire | Minderheitsinteresse |
| mint | Hôtel de la Monnaie | Münzprägeanstalt |
| money | monnaie | Geld |
| monopoly | monopole | Monopol |
| mortgage | hypothèque | Hypothek |
| **national debt** | dette nationale | Staatsschuld |
| national income | revenue nationale | Nationaleinkommen |
| nationalization | nationalisation | Verstaatlichung |
| net | net | netto, rein |

| English | French | German |
|---|---|---|
| net assets | valeurs nettes | netto Aktiva |
| new issue | nouvelle émission | Neuausgabe, Neuemission |
| news | nouvelles | Nachrichten, Neuigkeiten |
| nominal value, par | valeur nominal, parité | Nennwert, Nominalwert |
| nominee | nominée | Strohmann |
| **obsolescence** | désuétude, péremption (droit) | Veraltung |
| offer, bid | offre | Angebot |
| offer for sale | offre pour d'achat (OPA) | Verkaufsangebot, Übernahmeangebot |
| open position | position ouverte | offene Position |
| opening prices | cours d'ouverture | Anfangskurs |
| operational research | recherche opérationelle | Unternehmensforschung |
| option | option | Option |
| order (commission) | commande | Auftrag |
|   (bill of delivery) | bon de livraison | Lieferschein, Auslieferungsaufträge |
|   standing order | ordre ouvert | ständiger Auftrag |
| organization and methods | méthodes et organisation | Organisation und Methoden |
| outlet, market | débouché | Verkaufsstätte, Absatzmarkt |
| outlook | perspective | Aussicht |
| output | production | Produktion |
| over-subscribed | sur-souscription | übergezeichnet |
| overdraft | découvert | Kontoüberziehung |
| overheads | frais généraux | Betriebsspesen, Betriebskosten |
| overtime | heures supplémentaires | Überstunden |
| **packaging** | emballage | Verpackung |
| par | pair, parité | pari, Nennwert |
| parity | parité | Parität |
| partnership | société en commandite | Teilhaberschaft |
| patent | brevet | Patent |
| pay agreement | accord de paiement | Lohnabkommen |
| pay-out ratio | taux de pay-out | Auszahlungsrelation |
| percentage | pourcentage | Prozentsatz |
| personnel | personnel | Personal |
| planning | planification | Planung, Bewirtschaftung, Planwirtschaft |
| portfolio | portefeuille | Portefeuille |
| power of attorney | procuration | Vollmacht |
| preferential forms | formules privilégiées | Vorzugsformulare |
| premium | prime | Aufgeld, Agio |
| price | prix | Preis |
|   market price | prix de marché | Kurs |
|   producers' price | prix à la production, prix à la base | Produzentenpreis |
|   reserve price | mise à prix, prix plafond | Mindestpreis |
|   retail price | prix au détail | Einzelhandelspreis |
|   trade price | prix marchand, prix de demi gros | Handelspreis |
|   wholesale price | prix de gros | Großhandelspreis |
| price-earnings ratio | taux de price-earnings, rapport cours/bénéfices | Preis-/Verdienst-Relation |
| primary product | matière première | Grundstoff |
| prior charge | charges prioritaires | Vorrangsbelastung |
| process control | contrôle de production | Verarbeitungskontrolle |
| production | production | Produktion |
|   mass production | production de masse | Massenproduktion |
| productivity | productivité | Produktivität, Produktionsfähigkeit |
| production coefficient | taux de production | Produktionskoeffizient |
| profit | bénéfices | Gewinn |
|   retained profit | bénéfices non distribués | einbehaltener Gewinn |
|   trading profit | bénéfices d'exploitation | Betriebsgewinn |
| profit margin | marge bénéficiaire | Gewinnspanne |
| profit sharing | participation aux bénéfices | Gewinnbeteiligung |
| profitability | rentabilité | Rentabilität |
| prospectus | prospectus | Prospekt |
| protection | protection | Zollschutz |
| provisional allotment letter | avis d'attribution provisoire | provisorische Zuteilung |
| proxy (person) | fondé de pouvoir | Stellvertreter, Bevollmächtigter |
|   (document) | procuration | Vollmachturkunde |
| public corporation | régie | öffentlich-rechtliche Körperschaft |
| public ownership | propriété de l'état | Staatsbesitz |
| punter | accompagnateur, boursicoteur | kleiner Börsenspekulant, Spieler |
| **quality control** | contrôle de qualité | Qualitätskontrolle |
| quote (trade) | contingent | Quote, Kontingent |
| import, quote | contingent d'importation | Einfuhrquote |
| quotation | cotation | Preisangabe, Kurs, Kursnotierung |

# Management-Vokabular / Management Vocabulary / Vocabulaire Commercial

| English | French | German |
|---|---|---|
| rate (exchange) | cours | Wechselkurs |
| (interest) | taux | Zinsfuß |
| (local tax) | impôt local sur l'habitation | Gemeindesteuer |
| bank rate | taux officiel (d'escompte) | Diskontsatz |
| exchange rate | taux de change | Devisenkurs, Wechselkurs |
| floating exchange rate | taux de change flottant | gleitender Wechselkurs |
| growth rate | taux de croissance | Wachstumsrate |
| price rate | tarif à pièce | Stücklohn |
| time rate | tarif horaire | Zeitlohn |
| ratio | ratio, rapport | Relation, Verhältnis |
| price-earnings ratio | rapport cours/bénéfices, taux de price-earnings | Preis/Verdienst-Relation |
| rationalization | rationalisation | Rationalisierung |
| raw materials | matières brutes | Rohstoffe, Grundmaterialien |
| real | réel, fixe | real |
| realize | réaliser | realisieren |
| rebate, discount | remise, escompte | Rabatt |
| receipt | reçu | Quittung |
| recession | récession | Rezession, Rückgang |
| redemption | amortissement (loan), rachat (shares) | Tilgung |
| redemption date | date du remboursement | Einlösungs-/Fälligkeitsdatum |
| redemption yield | rendement sur remboursement | Einlösungsrendite |
| reflation | réflation | Re-Inflation |
| regulations | règlement | Regeln, Vorschriften |
| resale price maintenance | maintien du prix de vente au détail | Preisbindung der zweiten Hand |
| research | recherche | Forschung |
| operational research | recherche opérationnelle | Betriebsforschung |
| reserves | réserves | Reserven, Rücklagen |
| reserve price | mise à prix plafond | Mindestpreis |
| resources | ressources | Mittel |
| restrictive practice | pratique restrictive | restriktive Praktiken |
| retail to retail | vendre au détail | vertreiben im Einzelverkauf |
| revaluation | réévaluation | Aufwertung |
| revenue reserves | réserves prises sur le revenu | Einnahmereserven |
| risk | risque | Risiko |
| royalty | droits d'auteur, redevance | Tantieme, Lizenzgebühr |
| salary | traitement | Gehalt |
| sale | vente | Verkauf |
| salvage (money) | prime de sauvetage, indemnité de sauvetage | Bergegeld |
| saving | épargne, économie | Sparen, Ersparnis |
| savings bank | caisse d'épargne | Sparkasse |
| securities | titres | Wertpapiere |
| settlement/account day | jour de liquidation | Verrechnungstag |
| share | action, titre, valeur | Aktie |
| cumulative preference share | action préférence cumulative | nachzugsberechtigte Vorzugsaktie |
| deferred (manager's, founder's) share | part bénéficiaire, action différée | an letzter Stelle dividendenberechtigte Gründeraktie |
| non-voting share | action sans droit voté | stimmrechtslose Aktie |
| ordinary share | action ordinaire | (Stamm-) Aktie |
| preference share | action préférentielle | Vorzugsaktie |
| share certificate | certificat d'action | Aktienzertifikat |
| shift (work) | équipe | Schicht |
| short term | à court terme | kurzfristig |
| shorts | titres à court terme | kurzfristige Wertpapiere |
| sinking fund | fonds d'amortissement | Tilgungsfonds |
| sliding scale | échelle mobile | gleitende Skala |
| social insurance (security) | sécurité sociale | Sozialversicherung |
| solvent | solvable | solvent, zahlungsfähig |
| speculation | spéculation | Spekulation |
| spending | dépenses | Ausgaben, verausgaben |
| spot | comptant | Kassa, sofort zahlbar |
| squeeze | resserrement (crédit), compression (personnel), bloquage (salariés) | Quetschung, Beschränkung |
| stag | loup | Spekulant, der Neuausgaben von Aktien kurzfristig aufkauft |
| stamp duty | droit de timbre | Stempelsteuer |
| standing order | ordre ouvert | ständiger Auftrag |
| stock (inventory) | stock | Inventar |
| (share capital) | valeurs, capital | Stammkapital |
| active stocks | valeurs actives | umsatzstarke Papiere |
| bearer stock | action au porteur | Inhaberaktie |
| buffer stock | inventaire tampon | Bufferstock |
| growth stock | valeur de croissance | Wachstumswert |
| mining stock | valeur minière | Montanaktie, Kux |
| registered stock | action nominative | Namenspapier, Namensaktie |
| watered stock | capital dilué | verwässerte Werte |
| stockbroker | agent de change | Börsenmakler |
| stock control | gestion de stocks | Lagerkontrolle |
| stock exchange | bourse des valeurs | Börse |
| stockholder | actionnaire | Wertpapierbesitzer, Aktionär |
| strike | grève | Streik |
| subsidy | subvention | Subvention |
| subsidiary | filiale | Tochtergesellschaft |
| subscription | souscription | Abonnement |
| substitute | produit de remplacement | Ersatz, Ersetzung |
| supplier | fournisseur | Lieferant |
| supply and demand | offre et demande | Angebot und Nachfrage |
| surcharge | surtaxe | Aufgeld |
| surplus | excédent | Überschuss |
| takeover | prise de contrôle | Übernahme |
| tap stock | fonds publics à disponibilité continue | kontinuierlich dem Markt zugeführte Staatsanleihe |
| tariff | droit de douane | Zolltarif |
| time rates | tarif horaire | Zeitlohn |
| tax | impôt | Steuer |
| capital gains tax | impôt sur la plus-value du capital | Kapitalzusatzsteuer |
| corporation tax | impôt sur les sociétés | Körperschaftssteuer |
| future tax reserve | réserve pour impôts futurs | Rückstellung für zukünftige Steuerbelastung |
| income tax | impôt sur le revenu | Einkommensteuer |
| pay-roll tax | impôt cédulaire, cédule | Lohnsummensteuer |
| purchase tax | taxe de luxe | Umsatzsteuer |
| selective employment tax | impôt sélectif sur l'emploi | Körperschaftssteuer |
| surtax (supertax) | surtaxe | Supertax |
| value added tax (VAT) | taxe à valeur ajoutée (TVA) | Wertzuwachssteuer, Mehrwertsteuer |
| withholding tax | impôt par prélèvement | Kapitalertragssteuer |
| tender (shares, goods) | offre | Ausschreibung |
| legal tender | monnaie légale | gesetzliches Zahlungsmittel |
| time and study | étude sur la rentabilité du travail | Zeit- und Leistungsstudie |
| trade | commerce | Handel |
| free trade | libre échange | Freihandel |
| trade balance | balance commerciale | Leistungsbilanz |
| invisible trade balance | balance commerciale invisible | Dienstleistungsbilanz |
| visible trade balance | balance commerciale visible | Handelsbilanz |
| trade cycle | cycle économique | Konjunkturzyklus |
| trade gap | déficit sur le commerce extérieur | Handelslücke |
| trade investments | investissements directs | Handelsinvestition |
| trade mark | marque de fabrique | Handelsmarke |
| trade price | prix marchand, prix de demigros | Handelspreis |
| trade union | syndicat | Gewerkschaft |
| trading profits | bénéfices d'exploitation | Handelsgewinne |
| transfer deed | acte de transfert | Übertragungs-, Auflassungsurkunde |
| trend | tendance | Tendenz |
| trust | trust | Trust |
| investment trust | société d'investissement | Investment-Trust |
| open-ended trust | SICAV (Société d'investissement à capital variable) | Investment-Fonds mit beliebiger Emissionshöhe |
| unit trust | SICAV | Unit-Trust |
| turn (jobber's) commission | commission | Maklerspanne |
| turnover | chiffre d'affaires | Umsatz |
| uncalled capital | capital non versé | nicht eingezahltes Kapital |
| undersubscribed | émission non couverte | nicht voll untergebracht |
| underwriter | assureur | Versicherer |
| unemployment | chômage | Arbeitslosigkeit |
| unit trust | SICAV | Unit-Trust |
| unquoted securities | titres non cotés | unnotierte Wertpapiere |
| unsecured | sans garantie | ungesichert |
| unsecured loan stock | titres d'emprunt non garantis | ungesicherte Anleihen |
| value | valeur | Vermögenswerte, Werte |
| break-up value | valeur de récupération | Liquidationswert |
| marginal value | valeur marginale | Grenzwert |
| nominal value | valeur nominale | Nominalwert, Nennwert |
| variable (adj.) | variable | veränderlich, variabel |
| (noun) | variation | Veränderung |
| viable | viable | lebensfähig |
| wage | salaire | Lohn |
| wholesale | en gros | im Großen, en gros, Großhandel |
| work-in-progress | en cours de fabrication | im Arbeitsprozess |
| work-study | étude du travail | Arbeitsstudie |
| working capital | fonds du roulement, capital d'exploitation | Betriebskapital |
| yield | revenu | Rendite |

# Birthdays Geburtstage Anniversaires Compleanni
# Verjaardagen Cumpleaños

| | January | February | March |
|---|---|---|---|
| 1 | | | |
| 2 | | | |
| 3 | | | |
| 4 | | | |
| 5 | | | |
| 6 | | | |
| 7 | | | |
| 8 | | | |
| 9 | | | |
| 10 | | | |
| 11 | | | |
| 12 | | | |
| 13 | | | |
| 14 | | | |
| 15 | | | |
| 16 | | | |
| 17 | | | |
| 18 | | | |
| 19 | | | |
| 20 | | | |
| 21 | | | |
| 22 | | | |
| 23 | | | |
| 24 | | | |
| 25 | | | |
| 26 | | | |
| 27 | | | |
| 28 | | | |
| 29 | | | |
| 30 | | | |
| 31 | | | |

# Compleanni Anniversaires Geburtstage **Birthdays**
## Cumpleaños Verjaardagen

| | April | May | June |
|---|---|---|---|
| 1 | | | |
| 2 | | | |
| 3 | | | |
| 4 | | | |
| 5 | | | |
| 6 | | | |
| 7 | | | |
| 8 | | | |
| 9 | | | |
| 10 | | | |
| 11 | | | |
| 12 | | | |
| 13 | | | |
| 14 | | | |
| 15 | | | |
| 16 | | | |
| 17 | | | |
| 18 | | | |
| 19 | | | |
| 20 | | | |
| 21 | | | |
| 22 | | | |
| 23 | | | |
| 24 | | | |
| 25 | | | |
| 26 | | | |
| 27 | | | |
| 28 | | | |
| 29 | | | |
| 30 | | | |
| 31 | | | |

# Birthdays Geburtstage Anniversaires Compleanni
## Verjaardagen Cumpleaños

| | July | August | September |
|---|---|---|---|
| 1 | | | |
| 2 | | | |
| 3 | | | |
| 4 | | | |
| 5 | | | |
| 6 | | | |
| 7 | | | |
| 8 | | | |
| 9 | | | |
| 10 | | | |
| 11 | | | |
| 12 | | | |
| 13 | | | |
| 14 | | | |
| 15 | | | |
| 16 | | | |
| 17 | | | |
| 18 | | | |
| 19 | | | |
| 20 | | | |
| 21 | | | |
| 22 | | | |
| 23 | | | |
| 24 | | | |
| 25 | | | |
| 26 | | | |
| 27 | | | |
| 28 | | | |
| 29 | | | |
| 30 | | | |
| 31 | | | |

# Compleanni Anniversaires Geburtstage **Birthdays**
## Cumpleaños Verjaardagen

| | October | November | December |
|---|---|---|---|
| 1 | | | |
| 2 | | | |
| 3 | | | |
| 4 | | | |
| 5 | | | |
| 6 | | | |
| 7 | | | |
| 8 | | | |
| 9 | | | |
| 10 | | | |
| 11 | | | |
| 12 | | | |
| 13 | | | |
| 14 | | | |
| 15 | | | |
| 16 | | | |
| 17 | | | |
| 18 | | | |
| 19 | | | |
| 20 | | | |
| 21 | | | |
| 22 | | | |
| 23 | | | |
| 24 | | | |
| 25 | | | |
| 26 | | | |
| 27 | | | |
| 28 | | | |
| 29 | | | |
| 30 | | | |
| 31 | | | |

# 2011 Holiday List Feiertage  Jours Fériés  Giorni Festivi  Dias Festivos Feestdagen

**January 2011**
January 1, 2011, *Saturday*
Kwanzaa ends, *USA*
New Year's Day • Neujahr • Nouvel An •
Nieuwjaar

January 2, 2011, *Sunday*
Berchtoldstag, *Switzerland*

January 3, 2011, *Monday*
Bank Holiday, *UK, N. Ireland, Scotland*

January 4, 2011, *Tuesday*
Bank Holiday, *Scotland*

January 6, 2011, *Thursday*
Epiphany • Heilige Drei Könige •
Epiphanie • Driekoningen

January 17, 2011, *Monday*
Martin Luther King, Jr.'s Birthday, *USA*

January 25, 2011, *Tuesday*
Burns Day, *Scotland*

January 26, 2011, *Wednesday*
Australia Day, *Australia*

January 31, 2011, *Monday*
Koningin Beatrix (1938), *Netherlands*

**February 2011**
February 2, 2011, *Wednesday*
Groundhog Day, *USA*

February 3, 2011, *Thursday*
Chinese (Lunar) New Year

February 6, 2011, *Sunday*
Waitangi Day, *New Zealand*

February 14, 2011, *Monday*
St. Valentine's Day • Valentinstag •
Saint-Valentin • Valentijnsdag • Valentijn

February 21, 2011, *Monday*
President's Day, *USA*

**March 2011**
March 1, 2011, *Tuesday*
St. David's Day, *Wales*

March 7, 2011, *Monday*
Rosenmontag, *Germany*

March 8, 2011, *Tuesday*
Fastnacht, *Germany*
Mardi Gras, *USA, Canada, France*

March 9, 2011, *Wednesday*
Ash Wednesday • Aschermittwoch •
Cendres • Aswoensdag

March 13, 2011, *Sunday*
Daylight Saving Time begins, *USA,
Canada*

March 17, 2011, *Thursday*
St. Patrick's Day, *N. Ireland,
Rep. of Ireland, USA*

March 19, 2011, *Saturday*
Josephstag, *USA*
Purim • Pourim (begins at sundown)

March 20, 2011, *Sunday*
Vernal Equinox • Frühlings-
Tagundnachtgleiche • Printemps
(23:31 Universal Time)

March 27, 2011, *Sunday*
Clocks forward one hour, *UK*
Begin Zomertijd, *Belgium, Netherlands*
Beginn der Sommerzeit, *Austria,
Germany, Switzerland*

**April 2011**
April 3, 2011, *Sunday*
Mothering Sunday (Mother's Day), *UK*

April 17, 2011, *Sunday*
Palm Sunday • Palmsonntag • Dimanche
des Rameaux • Palmzondag •
Palm Pasen

April 18, 2011, *Monday*
Passover • Pessa'h (begins at sundown)

April 21, 2011, *Thursday*
Gründonnerstag, *Germany*
Witte Donderdag, *Netherlands*

April 22, 2011, *Friday*
Good Friday • Karfreitag • Vendredi
Saint • Goede Vrijdag
Orthodox Good Friday
Bank Holiday, *UK*

April 23, 2011, *Saturday*
St. George's Day, *England*

April 24, 2011, *Sunday*
Easter Sunday • Ostersonntag • Pâques •
Eerste Paasdag • Pasen
Orthodox Easter Sunday

April 25, 2011, *Monday*
Anzac Day, *Australia, New Zealand*
Easter Monday • Ostermontag •
Lundi de Pâques • Tweede Paasdag •
Paasmaandag
Bank Holiday, *UK*

April 27, 2011, *Wednesday*
Prins Willem Alexander (1967),
*Netherlands*

April 30, 2011, *Saturday*
Koninginnedag, *Netherlands*
Holocaust Remembrance Day •
Yom Hashoah (begins at sundown)

**May 2011**
May 1, 2011, *Sunday*
Dag van de arbeid, *Netherlands*
Feest van de Arbeid, *Belgium*
Fête du travail, *France*
Maifeiertag, *Germany*
Staatsfeiertag, *Austria*
Tag der Arbeit, *Switzerland*

May 2, 2011, *Monday*
May Day Bank Holiday, *UK,
Rep. of Ireland, Australia*

May 4, 2011, *Wednesday*
Herdenking der gevallenen, *Netherlands*

May 5, 2011, *Thursday*
Bevrijdingsdag, *Netherlands*

May 8, 2011, *Sunday*
Fête de la Victoire 1945, *France*
Mother's Day • Muttertag • Moederdag
Yom Ha'atzmaut (begins at sundown)

May 23, 2011, *Monday*
Victoria Day, *Canada*

May 29, 2011, *Sunday*
Fête des Mères, *France*

May 30, 2011, *Monday*
Memorial Day, *USA*
Spring Bank Holiday, *UK*

**June 2011**
June 2, 2011, *Thursday*
Ascension Day • Christi Himmelfahrt •
Ascension • Hemelvaartsdag • Onze
Lieve Heer – Hemelvaart • Auffahrt

June 6, 2011, *Monday*
Bank Holiday, *Rep. of Ireland*
Queen's Birthday, *New Zealand*

June 7, 2011, *Tuesday*
Shavuoth • Chavouoth
(begins at sundown)

June 12, 2011, *Sunday*
Pentecost Sunday • Pfingstsonntag •
Pentecôte • Eerste Pinksterdag •
Pinksteren

June 13, 2011, *Monday*
Pentecost Monday • Pfingstmontag •
Lundi de Pentecôte • Tweede
Pinksterdag • Pinkstermaandag

June 19, 2011, *Sunday*
Father's Day • Fête des Pères •
Vaderdag

June 21, 2011, *Tuesday*
Summer Solstice •
Sommersonnenwende • Solstice d'été
(17:16 Universal Time)

June 23, 2011, *Thursday*
Fronleichnam, *Austria, Germany,
Switzerland*

June 24, 2011, *Friday*
St. Jean Baptiste Day, *Canada (Quebec)*

**July 2011**
July 1, 2011, *Friday*
Canada Day, *Canada*

July 4, 2011, *Monday*
Independence Day, *USA*

July 12, 2011, *Tuesday*
Battle of the Boyne (Orangemen's Day),
*N. Ireland*

July 14, 2011, *Thursday*
Fête Nationale, *France*

July 21, 2011, *Thursday*
Nationale Feestdag, *Belgium*

**August 2011**
August 1, 2011, *Monday*
Nationalfeiertag, *Switzerland*
Bank Holiday, *Rep. of Ireland, Scotland*

August 8, 2011, *Monday*
Tisha B'Av (begins at sundown)

August 15, 2011, *Monday*
Feast of the Assumption •
Mariä Himmelfahrt • Assomption •
Maria ten hemelopneming •
Onze Lieve Vrouw – Hemelvaart

August 29, 2011, *Monday*
Summer Bank Holiday, *UK*
(except Scotland)

**September 2011**
September 5, 2011, *Monday*
Labor Day, *USA*
Labour Day, *Canada*

September 21, 2011, *Wednesday*
U.N. International Day of Peace

September 23, 2011, *Friday*
Autumnal Equinox • Herbst-
Tagundnachtgleiche • Automne
(09:04 Universal Time)

September 28, 2011, *Wednesday*
Rosh Hashanah • Roch Hachana
(begins at sundown)

**October 2011**
October 2, 2011, *Sunday*
Erntedankfest, *Germany*

October 3, 2011, *Monday*
Tag der Deutschen Einheit, *Germany*

October 7, 2011, *Friday*
Yom Kippur • Yom Kippour
(begins at sundown)

October 10, 2011, *Monday*
Columbus Day, *USA*
Thanksgiving Day, *Canada*

October 12, 2011, *Wednesday*
Sukkot • Souccot (begins at sundown)

October 19, 2011, *Wednesday*
Shemini Atzeret (begins at sundown)

October 20, 2011, *Thursday*
Simhat Torah (begins at sundown)

October 24, 2011, *Monday*
Labour Day, *New Zealand*

October 26, 2011, *Wednesday*
Nationalfeiertag, *Austria*

October 30, 2011, *Sunday*
Clocks back one hour, *UK*
Einde Zomertijd, *Belgium, Netherlands*
Ende der Sommerzeit, *Austria, Germany,
Switzerland*

October 31, 2011, *Monday*
Reformationstag, *Germany*
Halloween, *USA , UK*
Bank Holiday, *Rep. of Ireland*

**November 2011**
November 1, 2011, *Tuesday*
All Saints' Day • Allerheiligen • Toussaint

November 2, 2011, *Wednesday*
Allerseelen, *Austria*
Allerzielen, *Netherlands, Belgium*

November 6, 2011, *Sunday*
Daylight Saving Time ends, *USA,
Canada*

November 11, 2011, *Friday*
Martinstag, *Germany*
Armistice de 1918, *France*
Remembrance Day, *Canada, Australia*
Veteran's Day, *USA*
Wapenstilstand 1918, *Belgium*

November 13, 2011, *Sunday*
Volkstrauertag, *Germany*
Remembrance Sunday, *UK*

November 16, 2011, *Wednesday*
Buß- und Bettag, *Germany*

November 20, 2011, *Sunday*
Totensonntag, *Germany*
Ewigkeitssonntag, *Austria*

November 24, 2011, *Thursday*
Thanksgiving Day, *USA*

November 30, 2011, *Wednesday*
St. Andrew's Day, *Scotland*

**December 2011**
December 5, 2011, *Monday*
Sinterklaasavond, *Netherlands*

December 6, 2011, *Tuesday*
Saint-Nicolas, *France*
Sint Nicolaas, *Netherlands, Belgium*

December 8, 2011, *Thursday*
Immaculate Conception •
Mariä Empfängnis •
Immaculée Conception •
Maria onbevlekt ontvangen

December 20, 2011, *Tuesday*
Hanukkah • Hannoucah
(begins at sundown)

December 22, 2011, *Thursday*
Winter Solstice • Wintersonnenwende •
Solstice d'hiver (05:30 Universal Time)

December 24, 2011, *Saturday*
Christmas Eve • Heiligabend • Veille de
Noël • Kerstavond

December 25, 2011, *Sunday*
Christmas Day • 1. Weihnachtstag •
Noël • Eerste Kerstdag • Kerstmis

December 26, 2011, *Monday*
Boxing Day, *Australia, Canada, UK*
Kwanzaa begins, *USA*
St. Stephen's Day • Stephanitag •
Stephanstag • 2. Weihnachtstag •
Tweede Kerstdag
Bank Holiday, *UK*

December 27, 2011, *Tuesday*
Bank Holiday, *UK*

December 31, 2011, *Saturday*
New Year's Eve • Silvester •
Saint-Sylvestre • Oudejaarsdag •
Oudejaarsavond

## January 2011

| S | M | T | W | T | F | S |
|---|---|---|---|---|---|---|
|   |   |   |   |   |   | 1 |
| 2 | 3 | 4 | 5 | 6 | 7 | 8 |
| 9 | 10 | 11 | 12 | 13 | 14 | 15 |
| 16 | 17 | 18 | 19 | 20 | 21 | 22 |
| 23 | 24 | 25 | 26 | 27 | 28 | 29 |
| 30 | 31 |   |   |   |   |   |

## February 2011

| S | M | T | W | T | F | S |
|---|---|---|---|---|---|---|
|   |   | 1 | 2 | 3 | 4 | 5 |
| 6 | 7 | 8 | 9 | 10 | 11 | 12 |
| 13 | 14 | 15 | 16 | 17 | 18 | 19 |
| 20 | 21 | 22 | 23 | 24 | 25 | 26 |
| 27 | 28 |   |   |   |   |   |

## March 2011

| S | M | T | W | T | F | S |
|---|---|---|---|---|---|---|
|   |   | 1 | 2 | 3 | 4 | 5 |
| 6 | 7 | 8 | 9 | 10 | 11 | 12 |
| 13 | 14 | 15 | 16 | 17 | 18 | 19 |
| 20 | 21 | 22 | 23 | 24 | 25 | 26 |
| 27 | 28 | 29 | 30 | 31 |   |   |

## April 2011

| S | M | T | W | T | F | S |
|---|---|---|---|---|---|---|
|   |   |   |   |   | 1 | 2 |
| 3 | 4 | 5 | 6 | 7 | 8 | 9 |
| 10 | 11 | 12 | 13 | 14 | 15 | 16 |
| 17 | 18 | 19 | 20 | 21 | 22 | 23 |
| 24 | 25 | 26 | 27 | 28 | 29 | 30 |

## May 2011

| S | M | T | W | T | F | S |
|---|---|---|---|---|---|---|
| 1 | 2 | 3 | 4 | 5 | 6 | 7 |
| 8 | 9 | 10 | 11 | 12 | 13 | 14 |
| 15 | 16 | 17 | 18 | 19 | 20 | 21 |
| 22 | 23 | 24 | 25 | 26 | 27 | 28 |
| 29 | 30 | 31 |   |   |   |   |

## June 2011

| S | M | T | W | T | F | S |
|---|---|---|---|---|---|---|
|   |   |   | 1 | 2 | 3 | 4 |
| 5 | 6 | 7 | 8 | 9 | 10 | 11 |
| 12 | 13 | 14 | 15 | 16 | 17 | 18 |
| 19 | 20 | 21 | 22 | 23 | 24 | 25 |
| 26 | 27 | 28 | 29 | 30 |   |   |

## July 2011

| S | M | T | W | T | F | S |
|---|---|---|---|---|---|---|
|   |   |   |   |   | 1 | 2 |
| 3 | 4 | 5 | 6 | 7 | 8 | 9 |
| 10 | 11 | 12 | 13 | 14 | 15 | 16 |
| 17 | 18 | 19 | 20 | 21 | 22 | 23 |
| 24 | 25 | 26 | 27 | 28 | 29 | 30 |
| 31 |   |   |   |   |   |   |

## August 2011

| S | M | T | W | T | F | S |
|---|---|---|---|---|---|---|
|   | 1 | 2 | 3 | 4 | 5 | 6 |
| 7 | 8 | 9 | 10 | 11 | 12 | 13 |
| 14 | 15 | 16 | 17 | 18 | 19 | 20 |
| 21 | 22 | 23 | 24 | 25 | 26 | 27 |
| 28 | 29 | 30 | 31 |   |   |   |

## September 2011

| S | M | T | W | T | F | S |
|---|---|---|---|---|---|---|
|   |   |   |   | 1 | 2 | 3 |
| 4 | 5 | 6 | 7 | 8 | 9 | 10 |
| 11 | 12 | 13 | 14 | 15 | 16 | 17 |
| 18 | 19 | 20 | 21 | 22 | 23 | 24 |
| 25 | 26 | 27 | 28 | 29 | 30 |   |

## October 2011

| S | M | T | W | T | F | S |
|---|---|---|---|---|---|---|
|   |   |   |   |   |   | 1 |
| 2 | 3 | 4 | 5 | 6 | 7 | 8 |
| 9 | 10 | 11 | 12 | 13 | 14 | 15 |
| 16 | 17 | 18 | 19 | 20 | 21 | 22 |
| 23 | 24 | 25 | 26 | 27 | 28 | 29 |
| 30 | 31 |   |   |   |   |   |

## November 2011

| S | M | T | W | T | F | S |
|---|---|---|---|---|---|---|
|   |   | 1 | 2 | 3 | 4 | 5 |
| 6 | 7 | 8 | 9 | 10 | 11 | 12 |
| 13 | 14 | 15 | 16 | 17 | 18 | 19 |
| 20 | 21 | 22 | 23 | 24 | 25 | 26 |
| 27 | 28 | 29 | 30 |   |   |   |

## December 2011

| S | M | T | W | T | F | S |
|---|---|---|---|---|---|---|
|   |   |   |   | 1 | 2 | 3 |
| 4 | 5 | 6 | 7 | 8 | 9 | 10 |
| 11 | 12 | 13 | 14 | 15 | 16 | 17 |
| 18 | 19 | 20 | 21 | 22 | 23 | 24 |
| 25 | 26 | 27 | 28 | 29 | 30 | 31 |

● = New Moon / Neumond / Nouvelle lune
☽ = First Quarter or Waxing Moon / Erstes Viertel, zunehmender Mond / Premier quartier, lune montante
○ = Full Moon / Vollmond / Pleine lune
☾ = Last Quarter or Waning Moon / Letztes Viertel, abnehmender Mond / Dernier quartier, lune descendante

Lunar phases noted in this calendar are presented in terms of Universal Time.
Unsere Angaben der Mondphasen beziehen sich auf die Universal Time.
Les phases lunaires que nous indiquons se basent sur le Temps Universel de Greenwich.

# December 2010 Dezember Décembre Dicembre Diciembre December
# January 2011 Januar Janvier Gennaio Enero Januari

**27** Monday
Montag
Lundi
Lunedì
Lunes
Maandag

### December 2010

| S | M | T | W | T | F | S |
|---|---|---|---|---|---|---|
|   |   |   | 1 | 2 | 3 | 4 |
| 5 | 6 | 7 | 8 | 9 | 10 | 11 |
| 12 | 13 | 14 | 15 | 16 | 17 | 18 |
| 19 | 20 | 21 | 22 | 23 | 24 | 25 |
| 26 | 27 | 28 | 29 | 30 | 31 | |

**28** Tuesday
Dienstag
Mardi
Martedì
Martes ☾
Dinsdag

Bank Holiday, *UK*

### January 2011

| S | M | T | W | T | F | S |
|---|---|---|---|---|---|---|
|   |   |   |   |   |   | 1 |
| 2 | 3 | 4 | 5 | 6 | 7 | 8 |
| 9 | 10 | 11 | 12 | 13 | 14 | 15 |
| 16 | 17 | 18 | 19 | 20 | 21 | 22 |
| 23 | 24 | 25 | 26 | 27 | 28 | 29 |
| 30 | 31 | | | | | |

**29** Wednesday
Mittwoch
Mercredi
Mercoledì
Miércoles
Woensdag

**30** Thursday
Donnerstag
Jeudi
Giovedì
Jueves
Donderdag

### February 2011

| S | M | T | W | T | F | S |
|---|---|---|---|---|---|---|
|   |   | 1 | 2 | 3 | 4 | 5 |
| 6 | 7 | 8 | 9 | 10 | 11 | 12 |
| 13 | 14 | 15 | 16 | 17 | 18 | 19 |
| 20 | 21 | 22 | 23 | 24 | 25 | 26 |
| 27 | 28 | | | | | |

**31** Friday
Freitag
Vendredi
Venerdì
Viernes
Vrijdag

New Year's Eve • Silvester • Saint-Sylvestre • Oudejaarsdag • Oudejaarsavond

**1** Saturday
Samstag
Samedi
Sabato
Sábado
Zaterdag

Kwanzaa ends, *USA*
New Year's Day • Neujahr • Nouvel An • Nieuwjaar

**2** Sunday
Sonntag
Dimanche
Domenica
Domingo
Zondag

Berchtoldstag, *Switzerland*

Week 52

# THE IRON CHEF AT HOME

*"Father was a tyrant."*

# Januari Enero Gennaio Janvier Januar January 2011

Monday **3**
Montag
Lundi
Lunedì
Lunes
Maandag

Bank Holiday, *UK, N. Ireland, Scotland*

Tuesday **4**
Dienstag
Mardi
Martedì
Martes
Dinsdag

Bank Holiday, *Scotland*

Wednesday **5**
Mittwoch
Mercredi
Mercoledì
Miércoles
Woensdag

Thursday **6**
Donnerstag
Jeudi
Giovedì
Jueves
Donderdag

Epiphany • Heilige Drei Könige • Epiphanie • Driekoningen

Friday **7**
Freitag
Vendredi
Venerdì
Viernes
Vrijdag

Saturday **8**
Samstag
Samedi
Sabato
Sábado
Zaterdag

Sunday **9**
Sonntag
Dimanche
Domenica
Domingo
Zondag

Week 1

**December 2010**

| S | M | T | W | T | F | S |
|---|---|---|---|---|---|---|
|   |   |   | 1 | 2 | 3 | 4 |
| 5 | 6 | 7 | 8 | 9 | 10 | 11 |
| 12 | 13 | 14 | 15 | 16 | 17 | 18 |
| 19 | 20 | 21 | 22 | 23 | 24 | 25 |
| 26 | 27 | 28 | 29 | 30 | 31 |   |

**January 2011**

| S | M | T | W | T | F | S |
|---|---|---|---|---|---|---|
|   |   |   |   |   |   | 1 |
| 2 | 3 | 4 | 5 | 6 | 7 | 8 |
| 9 | 10 | 11 | 12 | 13 | 14 | 15 |
| 16 | 17 | 18 | 19 | 20 | 21 | 22 |
| 23 | 24 | 25 | 26 | 27 | 28 | 29 |
| 30 | 31 |   |   |   |   |   |

**February 2011**

| S | M | T | W | T | F | S |
|---|---|---|---|---|---|---|
|   |   | 1 | 2 | 3 | 4 | 5 |
| 6 | 7 | 8 | 9 | 10 | 11 | 12 |
| 13 | 14 | 15 | 16 | 17 | 18 | 19 |
| 20 | 21 | 22 | 23 | 24 | 25 | 26 |
| 27 | 28 |   |   |   |   |   |

# January 2011 Januar Janvier Gennaio Enero Januari

**10** Monday
Montag
Lundi
Lunedì
Lunes
Maandag

**11** Tuesday
Dienstag
Mardi
Martedì
Martes
Dinsdag

**December 2010**

| S | M | T | W | T | F | S |
|---|---|---|---|---|---|---|
|   |   |   | 1 | 2 | 3 | 4 |
| 5 | 6 | 7 | 8 | 9 | 10 | 11 |
| 12 | 13 | 14 | 15 | 16 | 17 | 18 |
| 19 | 20 | 21 | 22 | 23 | 24 | 25 |
| 26 | 27 | 28 | 29 | 30 | 31 |   |

**12** Wednesday
Mittwoch
Mercredi
Mercoledì
Miércoles
Woensdag                ☽

**January 2011**

| S | M | T | W | T | F | S |
|---|---|---|---|---|---|---|
|   |   |   |   |   |   | 1 |
| 2 | 3 | 4 | 5 | 6 | 7 | 8 |
| 9 | 10 | 11 | 12 | 13 | 14 | 15 |
| 16 | 17 | 18 | 19 | 20 | 21 | 22 |
| 23 | 24 | 25 | 26 | 27 | 28 | 29 |
| 30 | 31 |   |   |   |   |   |

**13** Thursday
Donnerstag
Jeudi
Giovedì
Jueves
Donderdag

**February 2011**

| S | M | T | W | T | F | S |
|---|---|---|---|---|---|---|
|   |   | 1 | 2 | 3 | 4 | 5 |
| 6 | 7 | 8 | 9 | 10 | 11 | 12 |
| 13 | 14 | 15 | 16 | 17 | 18 | 19 |
| 20 | 21 | 22 | 23 | 24 | 25 | 26 |
| 27 | 28 |   |   |   |   |   |

**14** Friday
Freitag
Vendredi
Venerdì
Viernes
Vrijdag

**15** Saturday
Samstag
Samedi
Sabato
Sábado
Zaterdag

**16** Sunday
Sonntag
Dimanche
Domenica
Domingo
Zondag

Week 2

Monday **17**
Montag
Lundi
Lunedì
Lunes
Maandag

Martin Luther King, Jr.'s Birthday, *USA*

Tuesday **18**
Dienstag
Mardi
Martedì
Martes
Dinsdag

### December 2010

| S | M | T | W | T | F | S |
|---|---|---|---|---|---|---|
| | | | 1 | 2 | 3 | 4 |
| 5 | 6 | 7 | 8 | 9 | 10 | 11 |
| 12 | 13 | 14 | 15 | 16 | 17 | 18 |
| 19 | 20 | 21 | 22 | 23 | 24 | 25 |
| 26 | 27 | 28 | 29 | 30 | 31 | |

Wednesday **19**
Mittwoch
Mercredi
Mercoledì
○ Miércoles
Woensdag

Tu Bishvat (begins at sundown)

### January 2011

| S | M | T | W | T | F | S |
|---|---|---|---|---|---|---|
| | | | | | | 1 |
| 2 | 3 | 4 | 5 | 6 | 7 | 8 |
| 9 | 10 | 11 | 12 | 13 | 14 | 15 |
| 16 | 17 | 18 | 19 | 20 | 21 | 22 |
| 23 | 24 | 25 | 26 | 27 | 28 | 29 |
| 30 | 31 | | | | | |

Thursday **20**
Donnerstag
Jeudi
Giovedì
Jueves
Donderdag

Friday **21**
Freitag
Vendredi
Venerdì
Viernes
Vrijdag

### February 2011

| S | M | T | W | T | F | S |
|---|---|---|---|---|---|---|
| | | 1 | 2 | 3 | 4 | 5 |
| 6 | 7 | 8 | 9 | 10 | 11 | 12 |
| 13 | 14 | 15 | 16 | 17 | 18 | 19 |
| 20 | 21 | 22 | 23 | 24 | 25 | 26 |
| 27 | 28 | | | | | |

Saturday **22**
Samstag
Samedi
Sabato
Sábado
Zaterdag

Sunday **23**
Sonntag
Dimanche
Domenica
Domingo
Zondag

Week 3

**24** Monday
Montag
Lundi
Lunedì
Lunes
Maandag

**December 2010**

| S | M | T | W | T | F | S |
|---|---|---|---|---|---|---|
|   |   |   | 1 | 2 | 3 | 4 |
| 5 | 6 | 7 | 8 | 9 | 10 | 11 |
| 12 | 13 | 14 | 15 | 16 | 17 | 18 |
| 19 | 20 | 21 | 22 | 23 | 24 | 25 |
| 26 | 27 | 28 | 29 | 30 | 31 |   |

**25** Tuesday
Dienstag
Mardi
Martedì
Martes
Dinsdag

Burns Day, *Scotland*

**26** Wednesday
Mittwoch
Mercredi
Mercoledì
Miércoles
Woensdag

☾

Australia Day, *Australia*

**January 2011**

| S | M | T | W | T | F | S |
|---|---|---|---|---|---|---|
|   |   |   |   |   |   | 1 |
| 2 | 3 | 4 | 5 | 6 | 7 | 8 |
| 9 | 10 | 11 | 12 | 13 | 14 | 15 |
| 16 | 17 | 18 | 19 | 20 | 21 | 22 |
| 23 | 24 | 25 | 26 | 27 | 28 | 29 |
| 30 | 31 |   |   |   |   |   |

**27** Thursday
Donnerstag
Jeudi
Giovedì
Jueves
Donderdag

**February 2011**

| S | M | T | W | T | F | S |
|---|---|---|---|---|---|---|
|   |   | 1 | 2 | 3 | 4 | 5 |
| 6 | 7 | 8 | 9 | 10 | 11 | 12 |
| 13 | 14 | 15 | 16 | 17 | 18 | 19 |
| 20 | 21 | 22 | 23 | 24 | 25 | 26 |
| 27 | 28 |   |   |   |   |   |

**28** Friday
Freitag
Vendredi
Venerdì
Viernes
Vrijdag

**29** Saturday
Samstag
Samedi
Sabato
Sábado
Zaterdag

**30** Sunday
Sonntag
Dimanche
Domenica
Domingo
Zondag

Week 4

# Januari Enero Gennaio Janvier Januar **January 2011**
# Februari Febrero Febbraio Février Februar **February 2011**

Monday **31**
Montag
Lundi
Lunedi
Lunes
Maandag

*Koningin Beatrix (1938), Netherlands*

Tuesday **1**
Dienstag
Mardi
Martedì
Martes
Dinsdag

*National Freedom Day, USA*

Wednesday **2**
Mittwoch
Mercredi
Mercoledì
Miércoles
Woensdag

*Groundhog Day, USA*

Thursday **3**
Donnerstag
Jeudi
Giovedì
Jueves
Donderdag

*Chinese (Lunar) New Year*

Friday **4**
Freitag
Vendredi
Venerdì
Viernes
Vrijdag

Saturday **5**
Samstag
Samedi
Sabato
Sábado
Zaterdag

Sunday **6**
Sonntag
Dimanche
Domenica
Domingo
Zondag

*Waitangi Day, New Zealand*

**Week 5**

**January 2011**

| S | M | T | W | T | F | S |
|---|---|---|---|---|---|---|
|   |   |   |   |   |   | 1 |
| 2 | 3 | 4 | 5 | 6 | 7 | 8 |
| 9 | 10 | 11 | 12 | 13 | 14 | 15 |
| 16 | 17 | 18 | 19 | 20 | 21 | 22 |
| 23 | 24 | 25 | 26 | 27 | 28 | 29 |
| 30 | 31 |   |   |   |   |   |

**February 2011**

| S | M | T | W | T | F | S |
|---|---|---|---|---|---|---|
|   |   | 1 | 2 | 3 | 4 | 5 |
| 6 | 7 | 8 | 9 | 10 | 11 | 12 |
| 13 | 14 | 15 | 16 | 17 | 18 | 19 |
| 20 | 21 | 22 | 23 | 24 | 25 | 26 |
| 27 | 28 |   |   |   |   |   |

**March 2011**

| S | M | T | W | T | F | S |
|---|---|---|---|---|---|---|
|   |   | 1 | 2 | 3 | 4 | 5 |
| 6 | 7 | 8 | 9 | 10 | 11 | 12 |
| 13 | 14 | 15 | 16 | 17 | 18 | 19 |
| 20 | 21 | 22 | 23 | 24 | 25 | 26 |
| 27 | 28 | 29 | 30 | 31 |   |   |

# February 2011 Februar Février Febbraio Febrero Februari

**7** Monday
Montag
Lundi
Lunedì
Lunes
Maandag

**8** Tuesday
Dienstag
Mardi
Martedì
Martes
Dinsdag

**9** Wednesday
Mittwoch
Mercredi
Mercoledì
Miércoles
Woensdag

**10** Thursday
Donnerstag
Jeudi
Giovedì
Jueves
Donderdag

**11** Friday
Freitag
Vendredi
Venerdì
Viernes
Vrijdag

**12** Saturday
Samstag
Samedi
Sabato
Sábado
Zaterdag

**13** Sunday
Sonntag
Dimanche
Domenica
Domingo
Zondag

## January 2011

| S | M | T | W | T | F | S |
|---|---|---|---|---|---|---|
|   |   |   |   |   |   | 1 |
| 2 | 3 | 4 | 5 | 6 | 7 | 8 |
| 9 | 10 | 11 | 12 | 13 | 14 | 15 |
| 16 | 17 | 18 | 19 | 20 | 21 | 22 |
| 23 | 24 | 25 | 26 | 27 | 28 | 29 |
| 30 | 31 |   |   |   |   |   |

## February 2011

| S | M | T | W | T | F | S |
|---|---|---|---|---|---|---|
|   |   | 1 | 2 | 3 | 4 | 5 |
| 6 | 7 | 8 | 9 | 10 | 11 | 12 |
| 13 | 14 | 15 | 16 | 17 | 18 | 19 |
| 20 | 21 | 22 | 23 | 24 | 25 | 26 |
| 27 | 28 |   |   |   |   |   |

## March 2011

| S | M | T | W | T | F | S |
|---|---|---|---|---|---|---|
|   |   | 1 | 2 | 3 | 4 | 5 |
| 6 | 7 | 8 | 9 | 10 | 11 | 12 |
| 13 | 14 | 15 | 16 | 17 | 18 | 19 |
| 20 | 21 | 22 | 23 | 24 | 25 | 26 |
| 27 | 28 | 29 | 30 | 31 |   |   |

Week 6

"Come along, son. We are at but the beginning of a
long and arduous journey."

*"I want you to have this. It belonged to my mother."*

# Februari Febrero Febbraio Février Februar **February 2011**

**Monday 14**
Montag
Lundi
Lunedì
Lunes
Maandag

St. Valentine's Day • Valentinstag • Saint-Valentin • Valentijnsdag • Valentijn

**Tuesday 15**
Dienstag
Mardi
Martedì
Martes
Dinsdag

**Wednesday 16**
Mittwoch
Mercredi
Mercoledì
Miércoles
Woensdag

**Thursday 17**
Donnerstag
Jeudi
Giovedì
Jueves
Donderdag

**Friday 18**
Freitag
Vendredi
Venerdì
Viernes
Vrijdag

**Saturday 19**
Samstag
Samedi
Sabato
Sábado
Zaterdag

**Sunday 20**
Sonntag
Dimanche
Domenica
Domingo
Zondag

## January 2011

| S | M | T | W | T | F | S |
|---|---|---|---|---|---|---|
|   |   |   |   |   |   | 1 |
| 2 | 3 | 4 | 5 | 6 | 7 | 8 |
| 9 | 10 | 11 | 12 | 13 | 14 | 15 |
| 16 | 17 | 18 | 19 | 20 | 21 | 22 |
| 23 | 24 | 25 | 26 | 27 | 28 | 29 |
| 30 | 31 |   |   |   |   |   |

## February 2011

| S | M | T | W | T | F | S |
|---|---|---|---|---|---|---|
|   |   | 1 | 2 | 3 | 4 | 5 |
| 6 | 7 | 8 | 9 | 10 | 11 | 12 |
| 13 | 14 | 15 | 16 | 17 | 18 | 19 |
| 20 | 21 | 22 | 23 | 24 | 25 | 26 |
| 27 | 28 |   |   |   |   |   |

## March 2011

| S | M | T | W | T | F | S |
|---|---|---|---|---|---|---|
|   |   | 1 | 2 | 3 | 4 | 5 |
| 6 | 7 | 8 | 9 | 10 | 11 | 12 |
| 13 | 14 | 15 | 16 | 17 | 18 | 19 |
| 20 | 21 | 22 | 23 | 24 | 25 | 26 |
| 27 | 28 | 29 | 30 | 31 |   |   |

Week 7

# February 2011 Februar Février Febbraio Febrero Februari

**21** Monday
Montag
Lundi
Lunedì
Lunes
Maandag

President's Day, *USA*

**22** Tuesday
Dienstag
Mardi
Martedì
Martes
Dinsdag

**23** Wednesday
Mittwoch
Mercredi
Mercoledì
Miércoles
Woensdag

**24** Thursday
Donnerstag
Jeudi
Giovedì
Jueves
Donderdag ☾

**25** Friday
Freitag
Vendredi
Venerdì
Viernes
Vrijdag

**26** Saturday
Samstag
Samedi
Sabato
Sábado
Zaterdag

**27** Sunday
Sonntag
Dimanche
Domenica
Domingo
Zondag

**January 2011**

| S | M | T | W | T | F | S |
|---|---|---|---|---|---|---|
| | | | | | | 1 |
| 2 | 3 | 4 | 5 | 6 | 7 | 8 |
| 9 | 10 | 11 | 12 | 13 | 14 | 15 |
| 16 | 17 | 18 | 19 | 20 | 21 | 22 |
| 23 | 24 | 25 | 26 | 27 | 28 | 29 |
| 30 | 31 | | | | | |

**February 2011**

| S | M | T | W | T | F | S |
|---|---|---|---|---|---|---|
| | | 1 | 2 | 3 | 4 | 5 |
| 6 | 7 | 8 | 9 | 10 | 11 | 12 |
| 13 | 14 | 15 | 16 | 17 | 18 | 19 |
| 20 | 21 | 22 | 23 | 24 | 25 | 26 |
| 27 | 28 | | | | | |

**March 2011**

| S | M | T | W | T | F | S |
|---|---|---|---|---|---|---|
| | | 1 | 2 | 3 | 4 | 5 |
| 6 | 7 | 8 | 9 | 10 | 11 | 12 |
| 13 | 14 | 15 | 16 | 17 | 18 | 19 |
| 20 | 21 | 22 | 23 | 24 | 25 | 26 |
| 27 | 28 | 29 | 30 | 31 | | |

Week 8

Monday **28**
Montag
Lundi
Lunedì
Lunes
Maandag

Tuesday **1**
Dienstag
Mardi
Martedì
Martes
Dinsdag

St. David's Day, *Wales*

**February 2011**

| S | M | T | W | T | F | S |
|---|---|---|---|---|---|---|
|   |   | 1 | 2 | 3 | 4 | 5 |
| 6 | 7 | 8 | 9 | 10 | 11 | 12 |
| 13 | 14 | 15 | 16 | 17 | 18 | 19 |
| 20 | 21 | 22 | 23 | 24 | 25 | 26 |
| 27 | 28 |   |   |   |   |   |

Wednesday **2**
Mittwoch
Mercredi
Mercoledì
Miércoles
Woensdag

**March 2011**

| S | M | T | W | T | F | S |
|---|---|---|---|---|---|---|
|   |   | 1 | 2 | 3 | 4 | 5 |
| 6 | 7 | 8 | 9 | 10 | 11 | 12 |
| 13 | 14 | 15 | 16 | 17 | 18 | 19 |
| 20 | 21 | 22 | 23 | 24 | 25 | 26 |
| 27 | 28 | 29 | 30 | 31 |   |   |

Thursday **3**
Donnerstag
Jeudi
Giovedì
Jueves
Donderdag

Friday **4**
Freitag
Vendredi
Venerdì
Viernes
Vrijdag

**April 2011**

| S | M | T | W | T | F | S |
|---|---|---|---|---|---|---|
|   |   |   |   |   | 1 | 2 |
| 3 | 4 | 5 | 6 | 7 | 8 | 9 |
| 10 | 11 | 12 | 13 | 14 | 15 | 16 |
| 17 | 18 | 19 | 20 | 21 | 22 | 23 |
| 24 | 25 | 26 | 27 | 28 | 29 | 30 |

Saturday **5**
Samstag
Samedi
Sabato
Sábado
Zaterdag

Sunday **6**
Sonntag
Dimanche
Domenica
Domingo
Zondag

Week 9

# March 2011 März Mars Marzo Marzo Maart

**7** Monday
Montag
Lundi
Lunedì
Lunes
Maandag

Rosenmontag, *Germany*

**8** Tuesday
Dienstag
Mardi
Martedì
Martes
Dinsdag

Fastnacht, *Germany*
Shrove Tuesday • Mardi Gras, *USA, Canada, France*

**9** Wednesday
Mittwoch
Mercredi
Mercoledì
Miércoles
Woensdag

Ash Wednesday • Aschermittwoch • Cendres • Aswoensdag

**10** Thursday
Donnerstag
Jeudi
Giovedì
Jueves
Donderdag

**11** Friday
Freitag
Vendredi
Venerdì
Viernes
Vrijdag

**12** Saturday
Samstag
Samedi
Sabato
Sábado
Zaterdag

☽

**13** Sunday
Sonntag
Dimanche
Domenica
Domingo
Zondag

Daylight Saving Time begins, *USA, Canada*

## February 2011

| S | M | T | W | T | F | S |
|---|---|---|---|---|---|---|
|   |   | 1 | 2 | 3 | 4 | 5 |
| 6 | 7 | 8 | 9 | 10 | 11 | 12 |
| 13 | 14 | 15 | 16 | 17 | 18 | 19 |
| 20 | 21 | 22 | 23 | 24 | 25 | 26 |
| 27 | 28 |   |   |   |   |   |

## March 2011

| S | M | T | W | T | F | S |
|---|---|---|---|---|---|---|
|   |   | 1 | 2 | 3 | 4 | 5 |
| 6 | 7 | 8 | 9 | 10 | 11 | 12 |
| 13 | 14 | 15 | 16 | 17 | 18 | 19 |
| 20 | 21 | 22 | 23 | 24 | 25 | 26 |
| 27 | 28 | 29 | 30 | 31 |   |   |

## April 2011

| S | M | T | W | T | F | S |
|---|---|---|---|---|---|---|
|   |   |   |   |   | 1 | 2 |
| 3 | 4 | 5 | 6 | 7 | 8 | 9 |
| 10 | 11 | 12 | 13 | 14 | 15 | 16 |
| 17 | 18 | 19 | 20 | 21 | 22 | 23 |
| 24 | 25 | 26 | 27 | 28 | 29 | 30 |

Week 10

# Maart Marzo Marzo Mars März March 2011

Monday **14**
Montag
Lundi
Lunedi
Lunes
Maandag

Tuesday **15**
Dienstag
Mardi
Martedì
Martes
Dinsdag

| **February 2011** | | | | | | |
|---|---|---|---|---|---|---|
| S | M | T | W | T | F | S |
| | | 1 | 2 | 3 | 4 | 5 |
| 6 | 7 | 8 | 9 | 10 | 11 | 12 |
| 13 | 14 | 15 | 16 | 17 | 18 | 19 |
| 20 | 21 | 22 | 23 | 24 | 25 | 26 |
| 27 | 28 | | | | | |

Wednesday **16**
Mittwoch
Mercredi
Mercoledì
Miércoles
Woensdag

| **March 2011** | | | | | | |
|---|---|---|---|---|---|---|
| S | M | T | W | T | F | S |
| | | 1 | 2 | 3 | 4 | 5 |
| 6 | 7 | 8 | 9 | 10 | 11 | 12 |
| 13 | 14 | 15 | 16 | 17 | 18 | 19 |
| 20 | 21 | 22 | 23 | 24 | 25 | 26 |
| 27 | 28 | 29 | 30 | 31 | | |

Thursday **17**
Donnerstag
Jeudi
Giovedì
Jueves
Donderdag

*St. Patrick's Day, N. Ireland, Rep. of Ireland, USA*

Friday **18**
Freitag
Vendredi
Venerdì
Viernes
Vrijdag

| **April 2011** | | | | | | |
|---|---|---|---|---|---|---|
| S | M | T | W | T | F | S |
| | | | | | 1 | 2 |
| 3 | 4 | 5 | 6 | 7 | 8 | 9 |
| 10 | 11 | 12 | 13 | 14 | 15 | 16 |
| 17 | 18 | 19 | 20 | 21 | 22 | 23 |
| 24 | 25 | 26 | 27 | 28 | 29 | 30 |

Saturday **19**
Samstag
Samedi
Sabato
Sábado
Zaterdag

○

*Josephstag, Switzerland*
Purim • Pourim (begins at sundown)

Sunday **20**
Sonntag
Dimanche
Domenica
Domingo
Zondag

Vernal Equinox • Frühlings-Tagundnachtgleiche • Printemps (23:31 Universal Time)

## Week 11

# March 2011 März Mars Marzo Marzo Maart

**21** Monday
Montag
Lundi
Lunedì
Lunes
Maandag

**February 2011**

| S | M | T | W | T | F | S |
|---|---|---|---|---|---|---|
| | | 1 | 2 | 3 | 4 | 5 |
| 6 | 7 | 8 | 9 | 10 | 11 | 12 |
| 13 | 14 | 15 | 16 | 17 | 18 | 19 |
| 20 | 21 | 22 | 23 | 24 | 25 | 26 |
| 27 | 28 | | | | | |

**22** Tuesday
Dienstag
Mardi
Martedì
Martes
Dinsdag

**March 2011**

| S | M | T | W | T | F | S |
|---|---|---|---|---|---|---|
| | | 1 | 2 | 3 | 4 | 5 |
| 6 | 7 | 8 | 9 | 10 | 11 | 12 |
| 13 | 14 | 15 | 16 | 17 | 18 | 19 |
| 20 | 21 | 22 | 23 | 24 | 25 | 26 |
| 27 | 28 | 29 | 30 | 31 | | |

**23** Wednesday
Mittwoch
Mercredi
Mercoledì
Miércoles
Woensdag

**April 2011**

| S | M | T | W | T | F | S |
|---|---|---|---|---|---|---|
| | | | | | 1 | 2 |
| 3 | 4 | 5 | 6 | 7 | 8 | 9 |
| 10 | 11 | 12 | 13 | 14 | 15 | 16 |
| 17 | 18 | 19 | 20 | 21 | 22 | 23 |
| 24 | 25 | 26 | 27 | 28 | 29 | 30 |

**24** Thursday
Donnerstag
Jeudi
Giovedì
Jueves
Donderdag

**25** Friday
Freitag
Vendredi
Venerdì
Viernes
Vrijdag

**26** Saturday
Samstag
Samedi
Sabato
Sábado
Zaterdag ☾

**27** Sunday
Sonntag
Dimanche
Domenica
Domingo
Zondag

Clocks forward one hour, *UK*
Begin Zomertijd, *Belgium, Netherlands*
Beginn der Sommerzeit, *Austria, Germany, Switzerland*

Week 12

"*Now close your eyes and go to sleep or Daddy will read you more of his novel.*"

"*That looks like fun.*"

Monday **28**
Montag
Lundi
Lunedì
Lunes
Maandag

Tuesday **29**
Dienstag
Mardi
Martedì
Martes
Dinsdag

| **March 2011** | | | | | | |
|---|---|---|---|---|---|---|
| S | M | T | W | T | F | S |
| | | 1 | 2 | 3 | 4 | 5 |
| 6 | 7 | 8 | 9 | 10 | 11 | 12 |
| 13 | 14 | 15 | 16 | 17 | 18 | 19 |
| 20 | 21 | 22 | 23 | 24 | 25 | 26 |
| 27 | 28 | 29 | 30 | 31 | | |

Wednesday **30**
Mittwoch
Mercredi
Mercoledì
Miércoles
Woensdag

| **April 2011** | | | | | | |
|---|---|---|---|---|---|---|
| S | M | T | W | T | F | S |
| | | | | | 1 | 2 |
| 3 | 4 | 5 | 6 | 7 | 8 | 9 |
| 10 | 11 | 12 | 13 | 14 | 15 | 16 |
| 17 | 18 | 19 | 20 | 21 | 22 | 23 |
| 24 | 25 | 26 | 27 | 28 | 29 | 30 |

Thursday **31**
Donnerstag
Jeudi
Giovedì
Jueves
Donderdag

| **May 2011** | | | | | | |
|---|---|---|---|---|---|---|
| S | M | T | W | T | F | S |
| 1 | 2 | 3 | 4 | 5 | 6 | 7 |
| 8 | 9 | 10 | 11 | 12 | 13 | 14 |
| 15 | 16 | 17 | 18 | 19 | 20 | 21 |
| 22 | 23 | 24 | 25 | 26 | 27 | 28 |
| 29 | 30 | 31 | | | | |

Friday **1**
Freitag
Vendredi
Venerdì
Viernes
Vrijdag

Saturday **2**
Samstag
Samedi
Sabato
Sábado
Zaterdag

Sunday **3**
Sonntag
Dimanche
Domenica
Domingo
Zondag

Mothering Sunday (Mother's Day), *UK*

Week 13

# April 2011 April Avril Aprile Abril April

**4** Monday
Montag
Lundi
Lunedì
Lunes
Maandag

**5** Tuesday
Dienstag
Mardi
Martedì
Martes
Dinsdag

**6** Wednesday
Mittwoch
Mercredi
Mercoledì
Miércoles
Woensdag

**7** Thursday
Donnerstag
Jeudi
Giovedì
Jueves
Donderdag

**8** Friday
Freitag
Vendredi
Venerdì
Viernes
Vrijdag

**9** Saturday
Samstag
Samedi
Sabato
Sábado
Zaterdag

**10** Sunday
Sonntag
Dimanche
Domenica
Domingo
Zondag

### March 2011

| S | M | T | W | T | F | S |
|---|---|---|---|---|---|---|
|   |   | 1 | 2 | 3 | 4 | 5 |
| 6 | 7 | 8 | 9 | 10 | 11 | 12 |
| 13 | 14 | 15 | 16 | 17 | 18 | 19 |
| 20 | 21 | 22 | 23 | 24 | 25 | 26 |
| 27 | 28 | 29 | 30 | 31 |   |   |

### April 2011

| S | M | T | W | T | F | S |
|---|---|---|---|---|---|---|
|   |   |   |   |   | 1 | 2 |
| 3 | 4 | 5 | 6 | 7 | 8 | 9 |
| 10 | 11 | 12 | 13 | 14 | 15 | 16 |
| 17 | 18 | 19 | 20 | 21 | 22 | 23 |
| 24 | 25 | 26 | 27 | 28 | 29 | 30 |

### May 2011

| S | M | T | W | T | F | S |
|---|---|---|---|---|---|---|
| 1 | 2 | 3 | 4 | 5 | 6 | 7 |
| 8 | 9 | 10 | 11 | 12 | 13 | 14 |
| 15 | 16 | 17 | 18 | 19 | 20 | 21 |
| 22 | 23 | 24 | 25 | 26 | 27 | 28 |
| 29 | 30 | 31 |   |   |   |   |

Week 14

# April Abril Aprile Avril April **April 2011**

Monday **11**
Montag
Lundi
Lunedì
Lunes
Maandag

Tuesday **12**
Dienstag
Mardi
Martedì
Martes
Dinsdag

| **March 2011** | | | | | | |
|---|---|---|---|---|---|---|
| S | M | T | W | T | F | S |
| | | 1 | 2 | 3 | 4 | 5 |
| 6 | 7 | 8 | 9 | 10 | 11 | 12 |
| 13 | 14 | 15 | 16 | 17 | 18 | 19 |
| 20 | 21 | 22 | 23 | 24 | 25 | 26 |
| 27 | 28 | 29 | 30 | 31 | | |

Wednesday **13**
Mittwoch
Mercredi
Mercoledì
Miércoles
Woensdag

| **April 2011** | | | | | | |
|---|---|---|---|---|---|---|
| S | M | T | W | T | F | S |
| | | | | | 1 | 2 |
| 3 | 4 | 5 | 6 | 7 | 8 | 9 |
| 10 | 11 | 12 | 13 | 14 | 15 | 16 |
| 17 | 18 | 19 | 20 | 21 | 22 | 23 |
| 24 | 25 | 26 | 27 | 28 | 29 | 30 |

Thursday **14**
Donnerstag
Jeudi
Giovedì
Jueves
Donderdag

Friday **15**
Freitag
Vendredi
Venerdì
Viernes
Vrijdag

| **May 2011** | | | | | | |
|---|---|---|---|---|---|---|
| S | M | T | W | T | F | S |
| 1 | 2 | 3 | 4 | 5 | 6 | 7 |
| 8 | 9 | 10 | 11 | 12 | 13 | 14 |
| 15 | 16 | 17 | 18 | 19 | 20 | 21 |
| 22 | 23 | 24 | 25 | 26 | 27 | 28 |
| 29 | 30 | 31 | | | | |

Saturday **16**
Samstag
Samedi
Sabato
Sábado
Zaterdag

Sunday **17**
Sonntag
Dimanche
Domenica
Domingo
Zondag

Palm Sunday • Palmsonntag • Dimanche des Rameaux •
Palmzondag • Palm Pasen

Week 15

**18** Monday
Montag
Lundi
Lunedì
Lunes ○
Maandag
Passover • Pessa'h (begins at sundown)

### March 2011

| S | M | T | W | T | F | S |
|---|---|---|---|---|---|---|
| | | 1 | 2 | 3 | 4 | 5 |
| 6 | 7 | 8 | 9 | 10 | 11 | 12 |
| 13 | 14 | 15 | 16 | 17 | 18 | 19 |
| 20 | 21 | 22 | 23 | 24 | 25 | 26 |
| 27 | 28 | 29 | 30 | 31 | | |

**19** Tuesday
Dienstag
Mardi
Martedì
Martes
Dinsdag

### April 2011

| S | M | T | W | T | F | S |
|---|---|---|---|---|---|---|
| | | | | | 1 | 2 |
| 3 | 4 | 5 | 6 | 7 | 8 | 9 |
| 10 | 11 | 12 | 13 | 14 | 15 | 16 |
| 17 | 18 | 19 | 20 | 21 | 22 | 23 |
| 24 | 25 | 26 | 27 | 28 | 29 | 30 |

**20** Wednesday
Mittwoch
Mercredi
Mercoledì
Miércoles
Woensdag

**21** Thursday
Donnerstag
Jeudi
Giovedì
Jueves
Donderdag
Gründonnerstag, Germany
Witte Donderdag, Netherlands

### May 2011

| S | M | T | W | T | F | S |
|---|---|---|---|---|---|---|
| 1 | 2 | 3 | 4 | 5 | 6 | 7 |
| 8 | 9 | 10 | 11 | 12 | 13 | 14 |
| 15 | 16 | 17 | 18 | 19 | 20 | 21 |
| 22 | 23 | 24 | 25 | 26 | 27 | 28 |
| 29 | 30 | 31 | | | | |

**22** Friday
Freitag
Vendredi
Venerdì
Viernes
Vrijdag
Good Friday • Karfreitag • Vendredi Saint • Goede Vrijdag
Orthodox Good Friday
Bank Holiday, UK

**23** Saturday
Samstag
Samedi
Sabato
Sábado
Zaterdag
St. George's Day, England

**24** Sunday
Sonntag
Dimanche
Domenica
Domingo
Zondag
Easter Sunday • Ostersonntag • Pâques • Eerste Paasdag • Pasen
Orthodox Easter Sunday

Week 16

Monday **25**
Montag
Lundi
Lunedì
Lunes
Maandag

Anzac Day, *Australia, New Zealand*
Easter Monday • Ostermontag • Lundi de Pâques • Tweede Paasdag • Paasmaandag
Bank Holiday, *UK*

Tuesday **26**
Dienstag
Mardi
Martedì
Martes
Dinsdag

| April 2011 | | | | | | |
|---|---|---|---|---|---|---|
| S | M | T | W | T | F | S |
| | | | | | 1 | 2 |
| 3 | 4 | 5 | 6 | 7 | 8 | 9 |
| 10 | 11 | 12 | 13 | 14 | 15 | 16 |
| 17 | 18 | 19 | 20 | 21 | 22 | 23 |
| 24 | 25 | 26 | 27 | 28 | 29 | 30 |

Wednesday **27**
Mittwoch
Mercredi
Mercoledì
Miércoles
Woensdag

Prins Willem Alexander (1967), *Netherlands*

| May 2011 | | | | | | |
|---|---|---|---|---|---|---|
| S | M | T | W | T | F | S |
| 1 | 2 | 3 | 4 | 5 | 6 | 7 |
| 8 | 9 | 10 | 11 | 12 | 13 | 14 |
| 15 | 16 | 17 | 18 | 19 | 20 | 21 |
| 22 | 23 | 24 | 25 | 26 | 27 | 28 |
| 29 | 30 | 31 | | | | |

Thursday **28**
Donnerstag
Jeudi
Giovedì
Jueves
Donderdag

| June 2011 | | | | | | |
|---|---|---|---|---|---|---|
| S | M | T | W | T | F | S |
| | | | 1 | 2 | 3 | 4 |
| 5 | 6 | 7 | 8 | 9 | 10 | 11 |
| 12 | 13 | 14 | 15 | 16 | 17 | 18 |
| 19 | 20 | 21 | 22 | 23 | 24 | 25 |
| 26 | 27 | 28 | 29 | 30 | | |

Friday **29**
Freitag
Vendredi
Venerdì
Viernes
Vrijdag

Saturday **30**
Samstag
Samedi
Sabato
Sábado
Zaterdag

Koninginnedag, *Netherlands*
Holocaust Remembrance Day • Yom Hashoah (begins at sundown)

Sunday **1**
Sonntag
Dimanche
Domenica
Domingo
Zondag

Dag van de arbeid, *Netherlands*
Feest van de Arbeid, *Belgium*
Fête du travail, *France*
Maifeiertag, *Germany*
Staatsfeiertag, *Austria*
Tag der Arbeit, *Switzerland*

Week 17

# May 2011 Mai Mai Maggio Mayo Mei

**2** Monday
Montag
Lundi
Lunedì
Lunes
Maandag

May Day Bank Holiday, *UK, Rep. of Ireland, Australia*

**3** Tuesday
Dienstag
Mardi
Martedì
Martes
Dinsdag ●

**4** Wednesday
Mittwoch
Mercredi
Mercoledì
Miércoles
Woensdag

Herdenking der gevallenen, *Netherlands*

**5** Thursday
Donnerstag
Jeudi
Giovedì
Jueves
Donderdag

Bevrijdingsdag, *Netherlands*

**6** Friday
Freitag
Vendredi
Venerdì
Viernes
Vrijdag

**7** Saturday
Samstag
Samedi
Sabato
Sábado
Zaterdag

**8** Sunday
Sonntag
Dimanche
Domenica
Domingo
Zondag

Fête de la Victoire 1945, *France*

Mother's Day • Muttertag • Moederdag
Yom HaAtzma'ut (begins at sundown)

## April 2011

| S | M | T | W | T | F | S |
|---|---|---|---|---|---|---|
|   |   |   |   |   | 1 | 2 |
| 3 | 4 | 5 | 6 | 7 | 8 | 9 |
| 10 | 11 | 12 | 13 | 14 | 15 | 16 |
| 17 | 18 | 19 | 20 | 21 | 22 | 23 |
| 24 | 25 | 26 | 27 | 28 | 29 | 30 |

## May 2011

| S | M | T | W | T | F | S |
|---|---|---|---|---|---|---|
| 1 | 2 | 3 | 4 | 5 | 6 | 7 |
| 8 | 9 | 10 | 11 | 12 | 13 | 14 |
| 15 | 16 | 17 | 18 | 19 | 20 | 21 |
| 22 | 23 | 24 | 25 | 26 | 27 | 28 |
| 29 | 30 | 31 |   |   |   |   |

## June 2011

| S | M | T | W | T | F | S |
|---|---|---|---|---|---|---|
|   |   |   | 1 | 2 | 3 | 4 |
| 5 | 6 | 7 | 8 | 9 | 10 | 11 |
| 12 | 13 | 14 | 15 | 16 | 17 | 18 |
| 19 | 20 | 21 | 22 | 23 | 24 | 25 |
| 26 | 27 | 28 | 29 | 30 |   |   |

Week 18

"*Remember, son, these are your tax-free years. Make the most of them.*"

"*Your early stuff was funnier.*"

Monday **9**
Montag
Lundi
Lunedì
Lunes
Maandag

Tuesday **10**
Dienstag
Mardi
Martedì
Martes
Dinsdag

☽

Wednesday **11**
Mittwoch
Mercredi
Mercoledì
Miércoles
Woensdag

Thursday **12**
Donnerstag
Jeudi
Giovedì
Jueves
Donderdag

Friday **13**
Freitag
Vendredi
Venerdì
Viernes
Vrijdag

Saturday **14**
Samstag
Samedi
Sabato
Sábado
Zaterdag

Sunday **15**
Sonntag
Dimanche
Domenica
Domingo
Zondag

| **April 2011** | | | | | | |
|---|---|---|---|---|---|---|
| S | M | T | W | T | F | S |
| | | | | | 1 | 2 |
| 3 | 4 | 5 | 6 | 7 | 8 | 9 |
| 10 | 11 | 12 | 13 | 14 | 15 | 16 |
| 17 | 18 | 19 | 20 | 21 | 22 | 23 |
| 24 | 25 | 26 | 27 | 28 | 29 | 30 |

| **May 2011** | | | | | | |
|---|---|---|---|---|---|---|
| S | M | T | W | T | F | S |
| 1 | 2 | 3 | 4 | 5 | 6 | 7 |
| 8 | 9 | 10 | 11 | 12 | 13 | 14 |
| 15 | 16 | 17 | 18 | 19 | 20 | 21 |
| 22 | 23 | 24 | 25 | 26 | 27 | 28 |
| 29 | 30 | 31 | | | | |

| **June 2011** | | | | | | |
|---|---|---|---|---|---|---|
| S | M | T | W | T | F | S |
| | | | 1 | 2 | 3 | 4 |
| 5 | 6 | 7 | 8 | 9 | 10 | 11 |
| 12 | 13 | 14 | 15 | 16 | 17 | 18 |
| 19 | 20 | 21 | 22 | 23 | 24 | 25 |
| 26 | 27 | 28 | 29 | 30 | | |

Week 19

# May 2011 Mai Mai Maggio Mayo Mei

**16** Monday
Montag
Lundi
Lunedì
Lunes
Maandag

**17** Tuesday
Dienstag
Mardi
Martedì
Martes
Dinsdag

**18** Wednesday
Mittwoch
Mercredi
Mercoledì
Miércoles
Woensdag

**19** Thursday
Donnerstag
Jeudi
Giovedì
Jueves
Donderdag

**20** Friday
Freitag
Vendredi
Venerdì
Viernes
Vrijdag

**21** Saturday
Samstag
Samedi
Sabato
Sábado
Zaterdag

Lag B'Omer (begins at sundown)
Armed Forces Day, *USA*

**22** Sunday
Sonntag
Dimanche
Domenica
Domingo
Zondag

## April 2011

| S | M | T | W | T | F | S |
|---|---|---|---|---|---|---|
|   |   |   |   |   | 1 | 2 |
| 3 | 4 | 5 | 6 | 7 | 8 | 9 |
| 10 | 11 | 12 | 13 | 14 | 15 | 16 |
| 17 | 18 | 19 | 20 | 21 | 22 | 23 |
| 24 | 25 | 26 | 27 | 28 | 29 | 30 |

## May 2011

| S | M | T | W | T | F | S |
|---|---|---|---|---|---|---|
| 1 | 2 | 3 | 4 | 5 | 6 | 7 |
| 8 | 9 | 10 | 11 | 12 | 13 | 14 |
| 15 | 16 | 17 | 18 | 19 | 20 | 21 |
| 22 | 23 | 24 | 25 | 26 | 27 | 28 |
| 29 | 30 | 31 |   |   |   |   |

## June 2011

| S | M | T | W | T | F | S |
|---|---|---|---|---|---|---|
|   |   |   | 1 | 2 | 3 | 4 |
| 5 | 6 | 7 | 8 | 9 | 10 | 11 |
| 12 | 13 | 14 | 15 | 16 | 17 | 18 |
| 19 | 20 | 21 | 22 | 23 | 24 | 25 |
| 26 | 27 | 28 | 29 | 30 |   |   |

Week 20

Monday **23**
Montag
Lundi
Lunedì
Lunes
Maandag

Victoria Day, *Canada*

Tuesday **24**
Dienstag
Mardi
Martedì
Martes
Dinsdag

Wednesday **25**
Mittwoch
Mercredi
Mercoledì
Miércoles
Woensdag

Thursday **26**
Donnerstag
Jeudi
Giovedì
Jueves
Donderdag

Friday **27**
Freitag
Vendredi
Venerdì
Viernes
Vrijdag

Saturday **28**
Samstag
Samedi
Sabato
Sábado
Zaterdag

Sunday **29**
Sonntag
Dimanche
Domenica
Domingo
Zondag

Fête des Mères, *France*

| April 2011 | | | | | | |
|---|---|---|---|---|---|---|
| S | M | T | W | T | F | S |
|  |  |  |  |  | 1 | 2 |
| 3 | 4 | 5 | 6 | 7 | 8 | 9 |
| 10 | 11 | 12 | 13 | 14 | 15 | 16 |
| 17 | 18 | 19 | 20 | 21 | 22 | 23 |
| 24 | 25 | 26 | 27 | 28 | 29 | 30 |

| May 2011 | | | | | | |
|---|---|---|---|---|---|---|
| S | M | T | W | T | F | S |
| 1 | 2 | 3 | 4 | 5 | 6 | 7 |
| 8 | 9 | 10 | 11 | 12 | 13 | 14 |
| 15 | 16 | 17 | 18 | 19 | 20 | 21 |
| 22 | 23 | 24 | 25 | 26 | 27 | 28 |
| 29 | 30 | 31 |  |  |  |  |

| June 2011 | | | | | | |
|---|---|---|---|---|---|---|
| S | M | T | W | T | F | S |
|  |  |  | 1 | 2 | 3 | 4 |
| 5 | 6 | 7 | 8 | 9 | 10 | 11 |
| 12 | 13 | 14 | 15 | 16 | 17 | 18 |
| 19 | 20 | 21 | 22 | 23 | 24 | 25 |
| 26 | 27 | 28 | 29 | 30 |  |  |

Week 21

# May 2011 Mai Mai Maggio Mayo Mei
# June 2011 Juni Juin Giugno Junio Juni

**30** Monday
Montag
Lundi
Lunedì
Lunes
Maandag — *Memorial Day, USA*
*Spring Bank Holiday, UK*

**May 2011**

| S | M | T | W | T | F | S |
|---|---|---|---|---|---|---|
| 1 | 2 | 3 | 4 | 5 | 6 | 7 |
| 8 | 9 | 10 | 11 | 12 | 13 | 14 |
| 15 | 16 | 17 | 18 | 19 | 20 | 21 |
| 22 | 23 | 24 | 25 | 26 | 27 | 28 |
| 29 | 30 | 31 | | | | |

**31** Tuesday
Dienstag
Mardi
Martedì
Martes
Dinsdag

**June 2011**

| S | M | T | W | T | F | S |
|---|---|---|---|---|---|---|
| | | | 1 | 2 | 3 | 4 |
| 5 | 6 | 7 | 8 | 9 | 10 | 11 |
| 12 | 13 | 14 | 15 | 16 | 17 | 18 |
| 19 | 20 | 21 | 22 | 23 | 24 | 25 |
| 26 | 27 | 28 | 29 | 30 | | |

**1** Wednesday
Mittwoch
Mercredi
Mercoledì
Miércoles
Woensdag

**July 2011**

| S | M | T | W | T | F | S |
|---|---|---|---|---|---|---|
| | | | | | 1 | 2 |
| 3 | 4 | 5 | 6 | 7 | 8 | 9 |
| 10 | 11 | 12 | 13 | 14 | 15 | 16 |
| 17 | 18 | 19 | 20 | 21 | 22 | 23 |
| 24 | 25 | 26 | 27 | 28 | 29 | 30 |
| 31 | | | | | | |

**2** Thursday
Donnerstag
Jeudi
Giovedì
Jueves
Donderdag — *Ascension Day • Christi Himmelfahrt • Ascension • Hemelvaartsdag •*
*Onze Lieve Heer – Hemelvaart • Auffahrt*

**3** Friday
Freitag
Vendredi
Venerdì
Viernes
Vrijdag

**4** Saturday
Samstag
Samedi
Sabato
Sábado
Zaterdag

**5** Sunday
Sonntag
Dimanche
Domenica
Domingo
Zondag

Week 22

# Juni Junio Giugno Juin Juni **June 2011**

## Monday Montag Lundi Lunedì Lunes Maandag — **6**

Bank Holiday, *Rep. of Ireland*
Queen's Birthday, *New Zealand*

## Tuesday Dienstag Mardi Martedì Martes Dinsdag — **7**

Shavuoth • Chavouoth (begins at sundown)

## Wednesday Mittwoch Mercredi Mercoledì Miércoles Woensdag — **8**

## Thursday Donnerstag Jeudi Giovedì Jueves Donderdag — **9**

## Friday Freitag Vendredi Venerdì Viernes Vrijdag — **10**

## Saturday Samstag Samedi Sabato Sábado Zaterdag — **11**

## Sunday Sonntag Dimanche Domenica Domingo Zondag — **12**

Pentecost Sunday • Pfingstsonntag • Pentecôte • Eerste
Pinksterdag • Pinksteren

**Week 23**

| **May 2011** | | | | | | |
|---|---|---|---|---|---|---|
| S | M | T | W | T | F | S |
| 1 | 2 | 3 | 4 | 5 | 6 | 7 |
| 8 | 9 | 10 | 11 | 12 | 13 | 14 |
| 15 | 16 | 17 | 18 | 19 | 20 | 21 |
| 22 | 23 | 24 | 25 | 26 | 27 | 28 |
| 29 | 30 | 31 | | | | |

| **June 2011** | | | | | | |
|---|---|---|---|---|---|---|
| S | M | T | W | T | F | S |
| | | | 1 | 2 | 3 | 4 |
| 5 | 6 | 7 | 8 | 9 | 10 | 11 |
| 12 | 13 | 14 | 15 | 16 | 17 | 18 |
| 19 | 20 | 21 | 22 | 23 | 24 | 25 |
| 26 | 27 | 28 | 29 | 30 | | |

| **July 2011** | | | | | | |
|---|---|---|---|---|---|---|
| S | M | T | W | T | F | S |
| | | | | | 1 | 2 |
| 3 | 4 | 5 | 6 | 7 | 8 | 9 |
| 10 | 11 | 12 | 13 | 14 | 15 | 16 |
| 17 | 18 | 19 | 20 | 21 | 22 | 23 |
| 24 | 25 | 26 | 27 | 28 | 29 | 30 |
| 31 | | | | | | |

# June 2011 Juni Juin Giugno Junio Juni

## May 2011

| S | M | T | W | T | F | S |
|---|---|---|---|---|---|---|
| 1 | 2 | 3 | 4 | 5 | 6 | 7 |
| 8 | 9 | 10 | 11 | 12 | 13 | 14 |
| 15 | 16 | 17 | 18 | 19 | 20 | 21 |
| 22 | 23 | 24 | 25 | 26 | 27 | 28 |
| 29 | 30 | 31 | | | | |

## June 2011

| S | M | T | W | T | F | S |
|---|---|---|---|---|---|---|
| | | | 1 | 2 | 3 | 4 |
| 5 | 6 | 7 | 8 | 9 | 10 | 11 |
| 12 | 13 | 14 | 15 | 16 | 17 | 18 |
| 19 | 20 | 21 | 22 | 23 | 24 | 25 |
| 26 | 27 | 28 | 29 | 30 | | |

## July 2011

| S | M | T | W | T | F | S |
|---|---|---|---|---|---|---|
| | | | | | 1 | 2 |
| 3 | 4 | 5 | 6 | 7 | 8 | 9 |
| 10 | 11 | 12 | 13 | 14 | 15 | 16 |
| 17 | 18 | 19 | 20 | 21 | 22 | 23 |
| 24 | 25 | 26 | 27 | 28 | 29 | 30 |
| 31 | | | | | | |

**13** Monday
Montag
Lundi
Lunedì
Lunes
Maandag

Pentecost Monday • Pfingstmontag • Lundi de Pentecôte • Tweede Pinksterdag • Pinkstermaandag

**14** Tuesday
Dienstag
Mardi
Martedì
Martes
Dinsdag

**15** Wednesday
Mittwoch
Mercredi
Mercoledì
Miércoles
Woensdag

**16** Thursday
Donnerstag
Jeudi
Giovedì
Jueves
Donderdag

**17** Friday
Freitag
Vendredi
Venerdì
Viernes
Vrijdag

**18** Saturday
Samstag
Samedi
Sabato
Sábado
Zaterdag

**19** Sunday
Sonntag
Dimanche
Domenica
Domingo
Zondag

Father's Day • Fête des Pères • Vaderdag

Week 24

"*That's my father. He's the understudy for my mother.*"

"It's O.K., kids—your mother's just having an argument."

Monday **20**
Montag
Lundi
Lunedì
Lunes
Maandag

Tuesday **21**
Dienstag
Mardi
Martedì
Martes
Dinsdag

Summer Solstice • Sommersonnenwende • Solstice d'été (17:16 Universal Time)

| May 2011 | | | | | | |
|---|---|---|---|---|---|---|
| **S** | **M** | **T** | **W** | **T** | **F** | **S** |
| 1 | 2 | 3 | 4 | 5 | 6 | 7 |
| 8 | 9 | 10 | 11 | 12 | 13 | 14 |
| 15 | 16 | 17 | 18 | 19 | 20 | 21 |
| 22 | 23 | 24 | 25 | 26 | 27 | 28 |
| 29 | 30 | 31 | | | | |

Wednesday **22**
Mittwoch
Mercredi
Mercoledì
Miércoles
Woensdag

| June 2011 | | | | | | |
|---|---|---|---|---|---|---|
| **S** | **M** | **T** | **W** | **T** | **F** | **S** |
| | | | 1 | 2 | 3 | 4 |
| 5 | 6 | 7 | 8 | 9 | 10 | 11 |
| 12 | 13 | 14 | 15 | 16 | 17 | 18 |
| 19 | 20 | 21 | 22 | 23 | 24 | 25 |
| 26 | 27 | 28 | 29 | 30 | | |

Thursday **23**
Donnerstag
Jeudi
Giovedì
Jueves
Donderdag

Fronleichnam, *Austria, Germany, Switzerland*

Friday **24**
Freitag
Vendredi
Venerdì
Viernes
Vrijdag

St. Jean Baptiste Day, *Canada (Quebec)*

| July 2011 | | | | | | |
|---|---|---|---|---|---|---|
| **S** | **M** | **T** | **W** | **T** | **F** | **S** |
| | | | | | 1 | 2 |
| 3 | 4 | 5 | 6 | 7 | 8 | 9 |
| 10 | 11 | 12 | 13 | 14 | 15 | 16 |
| 17 | 18 | 19 | 20 | 21 | 22 | 23 |
| 24 | 25 | 26 | 27 | 28 | 29 | 30 |
| 31 | | | | | | |

Saturday **25**
Samstag
Samedi
Sabato
Sábado
Zaterdag

Sunday **26**
Sonntag
Dimanche
Domenica
Domingo
Zondag

Week 25

# June 2011 Juni Juin Giugno Junio Juni
# July 2011 Juli Juillet Luglio Julio Juli

**27** Monday
Montag
Lundi
Lunedì
Lunes
Maandag

### June 2011

| S | M | T | W | T | F | S |
|---|---|---|---|---|---|---|
|   |   |   | 1 | 2 | 3 | 4 |
| 5 | 6 | 7 | 8 | 9 | 10 | 11 |
| 12 | 13 | 14 | 15 | 16 | 17 | 18 |
| 19 | 20 | 21 | 22 | 23 | 24 | 25 |
| 26 | 27 | 28 | 29 | 30 |   |   |

**28** Tuesday
Dienstag
Mardi
Martedì
Martes
Dinsdag

### July 2011

| S | M | T | W | T | F | S |
|---|---|---|---|---|---|---|
|   |   |   |   |   | 1 | 2 |
| 3 | 4 | 5 | 6 | 7 | 8 | 9 |
| 10 | 11 | 12 | 13 | 14 | 15 | 16 |
| 17 | 18 | 19 | 20 | 21 | 22 | 23 |
| 24 | 25 | 26 | 27 | 28 | 29 | 30 |
| 31 |   |   |   |   |   |   |

**29** Wednesday
Mittwoch
Mercredi
Mercoledì
Miércoles
Woensdag

**30** Thursday
Donnerstag
Jeudi
Giovedì
Jueves
Donderdag

### August 2011

| S | M | T | W | T | F | S |
|---|---|---|---|---|---|---|
|   | 1 | 2 | 3 | 4 | 5 | 6 |
| 7 | 8 | 9 | 10 | 11 | 12 | 13 |
| 14 | 15 | 16 | 17 | 18 | 19 | 20 |
| 21 | 22 | 23 | 24 | 25 | 26 | 27 |
| 28 | 29 | 30 | 31 |   |   |   |

**1** Friday
Freitag
Vendredi
Venerdì
Viernes
Vrijdag

● Canada Day, *Canada*

**2** Saturday
Samstag
Samedi
Sabato
Sábado
Zaterdag

**3** Sunday
Sonntag
Dimanche
Domenica
Domingo
Zondag

Week 26

Monday **4**
Montag
Lundi
Lunedì
Lunes
Maandag

*Independence Day, USA*

Tuesday **5**
Dienstag
Mardi
Martedì
Martes
Dinsdag

Wednesday **6**
Mittwoch
Mercredi
Mercoledì
Miércoles
Woensdag

Thursday **7**
Donnerstag
Jeudi
Giovedì
Jueves
Donderdag

Friday **8**
Freitag
Vendredi
Venerdì
Viernes
Vrijdag

Saturday **9**
Samstag
Samedi
Sabato
Sábado
Zaterdag

Sunday **10**
Sonntag
Dimanche
Domenica
Domingo
Zondag

| **June 2011** | | | | | | |
|---|---|---|---|---|---|---|
| S | M | T | W | T | F | S |
| | | | 1 | 2 | 3 | 4 |
| 5 | 6 | 7 | 8 | 9 | 10 | 11 |
| 12 | 13 | 14 | 15 | 16 | 17 | 18 |
| 19 | 20 | 21 | 22 | 23 | 24 | 25 |
| 26 | 27 | 28 | 29 | 30 | | |

| **July 2011** | | | | | | |
|---|---|---|---|---|---|---|
| S | M | T | W | T | F | S |
| | | | | | 1 | 2 |
| 3 | 4 | 5 | 6 | 7 | 8 | 9 |
| 10 | 11 | 12 | 13 | 14 | 15 | 16 |
| 17 | 18 | 19 | 20 | 21 | 22 | 23 |
| 24 | 25 | 26 | 27 | 28 | 29 | 30 |
| 31 | | | | | | |

| **August 2011** | | | | | | |
|---|---|---|---|---|---|---|
| S | M | T | W | T | F | S |
| | 1 | 2 | 3 | 4 | 5 | 6 |
| 7 | 8 | 9 | 10 | 11 | 12 | 13 |
| 14 | 15 | 16 | 17 | 18 | 19 | 20 |
| 21 | 22 | 23 | 24 | 25 | 26 | 27 |
| 28 | 29 | 30 | 31 | | | |

Week 27

# July 2011 Juli Juillet Luglio Julio Juli

**11** Monday
Montag
Lundi
Lunedì
Lunes
Maandag

**12** Tuesday
Dienstag
Mardi
Martedì
Martes
Dinsdag

Battle of the Boyne (Orangemen's Day), *N. Ireland*

**13** Wednesday
Mittwoch
Mercredi
Mercoledì
Miércoles
Woensdag

**14** Thursday
Donnerstag
Jeudi
Giovedì
Jueves
Donderdag

Fête Nationale, *France*

**15** Friday
Freitag
Vendredi
Venerdì
Viernes
Vrijdag

**16** Saturday
Samstag
Samedi
Sabato
Sábado
Zaterdag

**17** Sunday
Sonntag
Dimanche
Domenica
Domingo
Zondag

## June 2011

| S | M | T | W | T | F | S |
|---|---|---|---|---|---|---|
| | | | 1 | 2 | 3 | 4 |
| 5 | 6 | 7 | 8 | 9 | 10 | 11 |
| 12 | 13 | 14 | 15 | 16 | 17 | 18 |
| 19 | 20 | 21 | 22 | 23 | 24 | 25 |
| 26 | 27 | 28 | 29 | 30 | | |

## July 2011

| S | M | T | W | T | F | S |
|---|---|---|---|---|---|---|
| | | | | | 1 | 2 |
| 3 | 4 | 5 | 6 | 7 | 8 | 9 |
| 10 | 11 | 12 | 13 | 14 | 15 | 16 |
| 17 | 18 | 19 | 20 | 21 | 22 | 23 |
| 24 | 25 | 26 | 27 | 28 | 29 | 30 |
| 31 | | | | | | |

## August 2011

| S | M | T | W | T | F | S |
|---|---|---|---|---|---|---|
| | 1 | 2 | 3 | 4 | 5 | 6 |
| 7 | 8 | 9 | 10 | 11 | 12 | 13 |
| 14 | 15 | 16 | 17 | 18 | 19 | 20 |
| 21 | 22 | 23 | 24 | 25 | 26 | 27 |
| 28 | 29 | 30 | 31 | | | |

Week 28

Monday **18**
Montag
Lundi
Lunedì
Lunes
Maandag

Tuesday **19**
Dienstag
Mardi
Martedì
Martes
Dinsdag

| June 2011 | | | | | | |
|---|---|---|---|---|---|---|
| S | M | T | W | T | F | S |
| | | | 1 | 2 | 3 | 4 |
| 5 | 6 | 7 | 8 | 9 | 10 | 11 |
| 12 | 13 | 14 | 15 | 16 | 17 | 18 |
| 19 | 20 | 21 | 22 | 23 | 24 | 25 |
| 26 | 27 | 28 | 29 | 30 | | |

Wednesday **20**
Mittwoch
Mercredi
Mercoledì
Miércoles
Woensdag

| July 2011 | | | | | | |
|---|---|---|---|---|---|---|
| S | M | T | W | T | F | S |
| | | | | | 1 | 2 |
| 3 | 4 | 5 | 6 | 7 | 8 | 9 |
| 10 | 11 | 12 | 13 | 14 | 15 | 16 |
| 17 | 18 | 19 | 20 | 21 | 22 | 23 |
| 24 | 25 | 26 | 27 | 28 | 29 | 30 |
| 31 | | | | | | |

Thursday **21**
Donnerstag
Jeudi
Giovedì
Jueves
Donderdag

Nationale Feestdag, *Belgium*

Friday **22**
Freitag
Vendredi
Venerdì
Viernes
Vrijdag

| August 2011 | | | | | | |
|---|---|---|---|---|---|---|
| S | M | T | W | T | F | S |
| | 1 | 2 | 3 | 4 | 5 | 6 |
| 7 | 8 | 9 | 10 | 11 | 12 | 13 |
| 14 | 15 | 16 | 17 | 18 | 19 | 20 |
| 21 | 22 | 23 | 24 | 25 | 26 | 27 |
| 28 | 29 | 30 | 31 | | | |

Saturday **23**
Samstag
Samedi
Sabato
Sábado
Zaterdag

Sunday **24**
Sonntag
Dimanche
Domenica
Domingo
Zondag

Week 29

# July 2011 Juli Juillet Luglio Julio Juli

**25** Monday
Montag
Lundi
Lunedì
Lunes
Maandag

## June 2011

| S | M | T | W | T | F | S |
|---|---|---|---|---|---|---|
|   |   |   | 1 | 2 | 3 | 4 |
| 5 | 6 | 7 | 8 | 9 | 10 | 11 |
| 12 | 13 | 14 | 15 | 16 | 17 | 18 |
| 19 | 20 | 21 | 22 | 23 | 24 | 25 |
| 26 | 27 | 28 | 29 | 30 |   |   |

**26** Tuesday
Dienstag
Mardi
Martedì
Martes
Dinsdag

## July 2011

| S | M | T | W | T | F | S |
|---|---|---|---|---|---|---|
|   |   |   |   |   | 1 | 2 |
| 3 | 4 | 5 | 6 | 7 | 8 | 9 |
| 10 | 11 | 12 | 13 | 14 | 15 | 16 |
| 17 | 18 | 19 | 20 | 21 | 22 | 23 |
| 24 | 25 | 26 | 27 | 28 | 29 | 30 |
| 31 |   |   |   |   |   |   |

**27** Wednesday
Mittwoch
Mercredi
Mercoledì
Miércoles
Woensdag

**28** Thursday
Donnerstag
Jeudi
Giovedì
Jueves
Donderdag

## August 2011

| S | M | T | W | T | F | S |
|---|---|---|---|---|---|---|
|   | 1 | 2 | 3 | 4 | 5 | 6 |
| 7 | 8 | 9 | 10 | 11 | 12 | 13 |
| 14 | 15 | 16 | 17 | 18 | 19 | 20 |
| 21 | 22 | 23 | 24 | 25 | 26 | 27 |
| 28 | 29 | 30 | 31 |   |   |   |

**29** Friday
Freitag
Vendredi
Venerdì
Viernes
Vrijdag

**30** Saturday
Samstag
Samedi
Sabato
Sábado
Zaterdag ●

**31** Sunday
Sonntag
Dimanche
Domenica
Domingo
Zondag

Week 30

THE MONSTER PAUSES IN HIS RAMPAGE
TO SEND DR. FRANKENSTEIN A GREETING CARD.

# Augustus Agosto Agosto Août August **August 2011**

**1**
Monday
Montag
Lundi
Lunedì
Lunes
Maandag

Nationalfeiertag, *Switzerland*
Bank Holiday, *Rep. of Ireland, Scotland*

**2**
Tuesday
Dienstag
Mardi
Martedì
Martes
Dinsdag

**3**
Wednesday
Mittwoch
Mercredi
Mercoledì
Miércoles
Woensdag

**4**
Thursday
Donnerstag
Jeudi
Giovedì
Jueves
Donderdag

**5**
Friday
Freitag
Vendredi
Venerdì
Viernes
Vrijdag

**6**
Saturday
Samstag
Samedi
Sabato
Sábado
Zaterdag

》

**7**
Sunday
Sonntag
Dimanche
Domenica
Domingo
Zondag

Week 31

# August 2011 August Août Agosto Agosto Augustus

**8** Monday
Montag
Lundi
Lunedì
Lunes
Maandag

Tisha B'Av (begins at sundown)

**9** Tuesday
Dienstag
Mardi
Martedì
Martes
Dinsdag

**10** Wednesday
Mittwoch
Mercredi
Mercoledì
Miércoles
Woensdag

**11** Thursday
Donnerstag
Jeudi
Giovedì
Jueves
Donderdag

**12** Friday
Freitag
Vendredi
Venerdì
Viernes
Vrijdag

**13** Saturday
Samstag
Samedi
Sabato
Sábado
Zaterdag
○

**14** Sunday
Sonntag
Dimanche
Domenica
Domingo
Zondag

## July 2011

| S | M | T | W | T | F | S |
|---|---|---|---|---|---|---|
|   |   |   |   |   | 1 | 2 |
| 3 | 4 | 5 | 6 | 7 | 8 | 9 |
| 10 | 11 | 12 | 13 | 14 | 15 | 16 |
| 17 | 18 | 19 | 20 | 21 | 22 | 23 |
| 24 | 25 | 26 | 27 | 28 | 29 | 30 |
| 31 |   |   |   |   |   |   |

## August 2011

| S | M | T | W | T | F | S |
|---|---|---|---|---|---|---|
|   | 1 | 2 | 3 | 4 | 5 | 6 |
| 7 | 8 | 9 | 10 | 11 | 12 | 13 |
| 14 | 15 | 16 | 17 | 18 | 19 | 20 |
| 21 | 22 | 23 | 24 | 25 | 26 | 27 |
| 28 | 29 | 30 | 31 |   |   |   |

## September 2011

| S | M | T | W | T | F | S |
|---|---|---|---|---|---|---|
|   |   |   |   | 1 | 2 | 3 |
| 4 | 5 | 6 | 7 | 8 | 9 | 10 |
| 11 | 12 | 13 | 14 | 15 | 16 | 17 |
| 18 | 19 | 20 | 21 | 22 | 23 | 24 |
| 25 | 26 | 27 | 28 | 29 | 30 |   |

Week 32

Monday **15**
Montag
Lundi
Lunedì
Lunes
Maandag

Feast of the Assumption • Mariä Himmelfahrt • Assomption • Maria ten hemelopneming •
Onze Lieve Vrouw – Hemelvaart

Tuesday **16**
Dienstag
Mardi
Martedì
Martes
Dinsdag

| July 2011 | | | | | | |
|---|---|---|---|---|---|---|
| S | M | T | W | T | F | S |
| | | | | | 1 | 2 |
| 3 | 4 | 5 | 6 | 7 | 8 | 9 |
| 10 | 11 | 12 | 13 | 14 | 15 | 16 |
| 17 | 18 | 19 | 20 | 21 | 22 | 23 |
| 24 | 25 | 26 | 27 | 28 | 29 | 30 |
| 31 | | | | | | |

Wednesday **17**
Mittwoch
Mercredi
Mercoledì
Miércoles
Woensdag

| August 2011 | | | | | | |
|---|---|---|---|---|---|---|
| S | M | T | W | T | F | S |
| | 1 | 2 | 3 | 4 | 5 | 6 |
| 7 | 8 | 9 | 10 | 11 | 12 | 13 |
| 14 | 15 | 16 | 17 | 18 | 19 | 20 |
| 21 | 22 | 23 | 24 | 25 | 26 | 27 |
| 28 | 29 | 30 | 31 | | | |

Thursday **18**
Donnerstag
Jeudi
Giovedì
Jueves
Donderdag

Friday **19**
Freitag
Vendredi
Venerdì
Viernes
Vrijdag

| September 2011 | | | | | | |
|---|---|---|---|---|---|---|
| S | M | T | W | T | F | S |
| | | | | 1 | 2 | 3 |
| 4 | 5 | 6 | 7 | 8 | 9 | 10 |
| 11 | 12 | 13 | 14 | 15 | 16 | 17 |
| 18 | 19 | 20 | 21 | 22 | 23 | 24 |
| 25 | 26 | 27 | 28 | 29 | 30 | |

Saturday **20**
Samstag
Samedi
Sabato
Sábado
Zaterdag

Sunday **21**
Sonntag
Dimanche
Domenica
Domingo
Zondag

Week 33

# August 2011 August Août Agosto Agosto Augustus

**22** Monday
Montag
Lundi
Lunedì
Lunes
Maandag

### July 2011

| S | M | T | W | T | F | S |
|---|---|---|---|---|---|---|
| | | | | | 1 | 2 |
| 3 | 4 | 5 | 6 | 7 | 8 | 9 |
| 10 | 11 | 12 | 13 | 14 | 15 | 16 |
| 17 | 18 | 19 | 20 | 21 | 22 | 23 |
| 24 | 25 | 26 | 27 | 28 | 29 | 30 |
| 31 | | | | | | |

**23** Tuesday
Dienstag
Mardi
Martedì
Martes
Dinsdag

**24** Wednesday
Mittwoch
Mercredi
Mercoledì
Miércoles
Woensdag

### August 2011

| S | M | T | W | T | F | S |
|---|---|---|---|---|---|---|
| | 1 | 2 | 3 | 4 | 5 | 6 |
| 7 | 8 | 9 | 10 | 11 | 12 | 13 |
| 14 | 15 | 16 | 17 | 18 | 19 | 20 |
| 21 | 22 | 23 | 24 | 25 | 26 | 27 |
| 28 | 29 | 30 | 31 | | | |

**25** Thursday
Donnerstag
Jeudi
Giovedì
Jueves
Donderdag

**26** Friday
Freitag
Vendredi
Venerdì
Viernes
Vrijdag

### September 2011

| S | M | T | W | T | F | S |
|---|---|---|---|---|---|---|
| | | | | 1 | 2 | 3 |
| 4 | 5 | 6 | 7 | 8 | 9 | 10 |
| 11 | 12 | 13 | 14 | 15 | 16 | 17 |
| 18 | 19 | 20 | 21 | 22 | 23 | 24 |
| 25 | 26 | 27 | 28 | 29 | 30 | |

**27** Saturday
Samstag
Samedi
Sabato
Sábado
Zaterdag

**28** Sunday
Sonntag
Dimanche
Domenica
Domingo
Zondag

Week 34

# Augustus Agosto Agosto Août August **August 2011**
# September Septiembre Settembre Septembre September **September 2011**

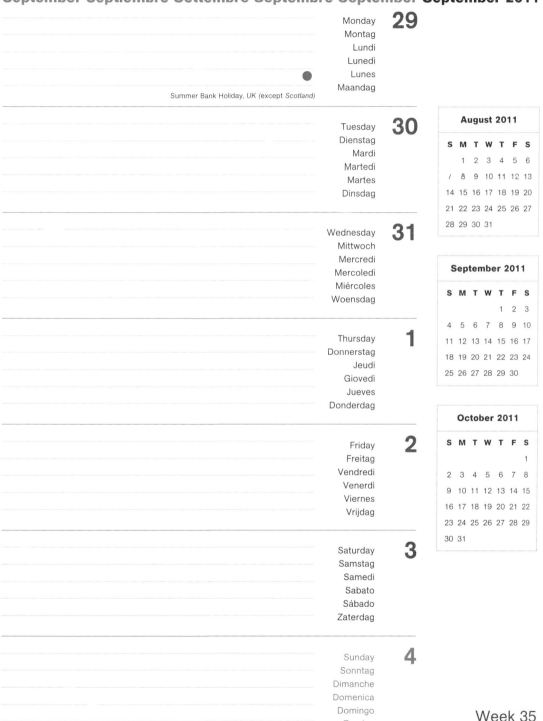

Monday / Montag / Lundi / Lunedi / Lunes / Maandag **29**

Summer Bank Holiday, *UK (except Scotland)*

Tuesday / Dienstag / Mardi / Martedi / Martes / Dinsdag **30**

| **August 2011** | | | | | | |
|---|---|---|---|---|---|---|
| S | M | T | W | T | F | S |
| | 1 | 2 | 3 | 4 | 5 | 6 |
| 7 | 8 | 9 | 10 | 11 | 12 | 13 |
| 14 | 15 | 16 | 17 | 18 | 19 | 20 |
| 21 | 22 | 23 | 24 | 25 | 26 | 27 |
| 28 | 29 | 30 | 31 | | | |

Wednesday / Mittwoch / Mercredi / Mercoledi / Miércoles / Woensdag **31**

| **September 2011** | | | | | | |
|---|---|---|---|---|---|---|
| S | M | T | W | T | F | S |
| | | | | 1 | 2 | 3 |
| 4 | 5 | 6 | 7 | 8 | 9 | 10 |
| 11 | 12 | 13 | 14 | 15 | 16 | 17 |
| 18 | 19 | 20 | 21 | 22 | 23 | 24 |
| 25 | 26 | 27 | 28 | 29 | 30 | |

Thursday / Donnerstag / Jeudi / Giovedi / Jueves / Donderdag **1**

Friday / Freitag / Vendredi / Venerdi / Viernes / Vrijdag **2**

| **October 2011** | | | | | | |
|---|---|---|---|---|---|---|
| S | M | T | W | T | F | S |
| | | | | | | 1 |
| 2 | 3 | 4 | 5 | 6 | 7 | 8 |
| 9 | 10 | 11 | 12 | 13 | 14 | 15 |
| 16 | 17 | 18 | 19 | 20 | 21 | 22 |
| 23 | 24 | 25 | 26 | 27 | 28 | 29 |
| 30 | 31 | | | | | |

Saturday / Samstag / Samedi / Sabato / Sábado / Zaterdag **3**

Sunday / Sonntag / Dimanche / Domenica / Domingo / Zondag **4**

Week 35

**5** Monday
Montag
Lundi
Lunedì
Lunes
Maandag  Labor Day, *USA*
Labour Day, *Canada*

## August 2011

| S | M | T | W | T | F | S |
|---|---|---|---|---|---|---|
|   | 1 | 2 | 3 | 4 | 5 | 6 |
| 7 | 8 | 9 | 10 | 11 | 12 | 13 |
| 14 | 15 | 16 | 17 | 18 | 19 | 20 |
| 21 | 22 | 23 | 24 | 25 | 26 | 27 |
| 28 | 29 | 30 | 31 |   |   |   |

**6** Tuesday
Dienstag
Mardi
Martedì
Martes
Dinsdag

## September 2011

| S | M | T | W | T | F | S |
|---|---|---|---|---|---|---|
|   |   |   |   | 1 | 2 | 3 |
| 4 | 5 | 6 | 7 | 8 | 9 | 10 |
| 11 | 12 | 13 | 14 | 15 | 16 | 17 |
| 18 | 19 | 20 | 21 | 22 | 23 | 24 |
| 25 | 26 | 27 | 28 | 29 | 30 |   |

**7** Wednesday
Mittwoch
Mercredi
Mercoledì
Miércoles
Woensdag

## October 2011

| S | M | T | W | T | F | S |
|---|---|---|---|---|---|---|
|   |   |   |   |   |   | 1 |
| 2 | 3 | 4 | 5 | 6 | 7 | 8 |
| 9 | 10 | 11 | 12 | 13 | 14 | 15 |
| 16 | 17 | 18 | 19 | 20 | 21 | 22 |
| 23 | 24 | 25 | 26 | 27 | 28 | 29 |
| 30 | 31 |   |   |   |   |   |

**8** Thursday
Donnerstag
Jeudi
Giovedì
Jueves
Donderdag

**9** Friday
Freitag
Vendredi
Venerdì
Viernes
Vrijdag

**10** Saturday
Samstag
Samedi
Sabato
Sábado
Zaterdag

**11** Sunday
Sonntag
Dimanche
Domenica
Domingo
Zondag

Week 36

"*This is a nice restaurant. Turn your cap around.*"

P. BYRNES.

"*Just remember, son, it doesn't matter whether you win or lose—unless you want Daddy's love.*"

Monday **12**
Montag
Lundi
Lunedi
Lunes
Maandag

Tuesday **13**
Dienstag
Mardi
Martedi
Martes
Dinsdag

| August 2011 | | | | | | |
|---|---|---|---|---|---|---|
| S | M | T | W | T | F | S |
| | 1 | 2 | 3 | 4 | 5 | 6 |
| 7 | 8 | 9 | 10 | 11 | 12 | 13 |
| 14 | 15 | 16 | 17 | 18 | 19 | 20 |
| 21 | 22 | 23 | 24 | 25 | 26 | 27 |
| 28 | 29 | 30 | 31 | | | |

Wednesday **14**
Mittwoch
Mercredi
Mercoledi
Miércoles
Woensdag

Thursday **15**
Donnerstag
Jeudi
Giovedi
Jueves
Donderdag

| September 2011 | | | | | | |
|---|---|---|---|---|---|---|
| S | M | T | W | T | F | S |
| | | | | 1 | 2 | 3 |
| 4 | 5 | 6 | 7 | 8 | 9 | 10 |
| 11 | 12 | 13 | 14 | 15 | 16 | 17 |
| 18 | 19 | 20 | 21 | 22 | 23 | 24 |
| 25 | 26 | 27 | 28 | 29 | 30 | |

Friday **16**
Freitag
Vendredi
Venerdi
Viernes
Vrijdag

| October 2011 | | | | | | |
|---|---|---|---|---|---|---|
| S | M | T | W | T | F | S |
| | | | | | | 1 |
| 2 | 3 | 4 | 5 | 6 | 7 | 8 |
| 9 | 10 | 11 | 12 | 13 | 14 | 15 |
| 16 | 17 | 18 | 19 | 20 | 21 | 22 |
| 23 | 24 | 25 | 26 | 27 | 28 | 29 |
| 30 | 31 | | | | | |

Saturday **17**
Samstag
Samedi
Sabato
Sábado
Zaterdag

Sunday **18**
Sonntag
Dimanche
Domenica
Domingo
Zondag

Week 37

**19** Monday
Montag
Lundi
Lunedì
Lunes
Maandag

**August 2011**

| S | M | T | W | T | F | S |
|---|---|---|---|---|---|---|
| | 1 | 2 | 3 | 4 | 5 | 6 |
| 7 | 8 | 9 | 10 | 11 | 12 | 13 |
| 14 | 15 | 16 | 17 | 18 | 19 | 20 |
| 21 | 22 | 23 | 24 | 25 | 26 | 27 |
| 28 | 29 | 30 | 31 | | | |

**20** Tuesday
Dienstag
Mardi
Martedì
Martes
Dinsdag

**September 2011**

| S | M | T | W | T | F | S |
|---|---|---|---|---|---|---|
| | | | | 1 | 2 | 3 |
| 4 | 5 | 6 | 7 | 8 | 9 | 10 |
| 11 | 12 | 13 | 14 | 15 | 16 | 17 |
| 18 | 19 | 20 | 21 | 22 | 23 | 24 |
| 25 | 26 | 27 | 28 | 29 | 30 | |

**21** Wednesday
Mittwoch
Mercredi
Mercoledì
Miércoles
Woensdag

U.N. International Day of Peace

**22** Thursday
Donnerstag
Jeudi
Giovedì
Jueves
Donderdag

**October 2011**

| S | M | T | W | T | F | S |
|---|---|---|---|---|---|---|
| | | | | | | 1 |
| 2 | 3 | 4 | 5 | 6 | 7 | 8 |
| 9 | 10 | 11 | 12 | 13 | 14 | 15 |
| 16 | 17 | 18 | 19 | 20 | 21 | 22 |
| 23 | 24 | 25 | 26 | 27 | 28 | 29 |
| 30 | 31 | | | | | |

**23** Friday
Freitag
Vendredi
Venerdì
Viernes
Vrijdag

Autumnal Equinox • Herbst-Tagundnachtgleiche • Automne (09:04 Universal Time)

**24** Saturday
Samstag
Samedi
Sabato
Sábado
Zaterdag

**25** Sunday
Sonntag
Dimanche
Domenica
Domingo
Zondag

Week 38

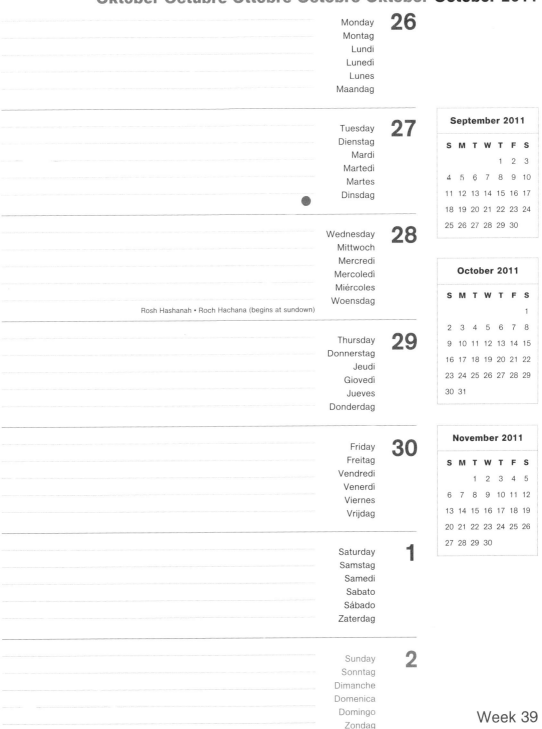

Monday **26**
Montag
Lundi
Lunedì
Lunes
Maandag

Tuesday **27**
Dienstag
Mardi
Martedì
Martes
Dinsdag

**September 2011**

| S | M | T | W | T | F | S |
|---|---|---|---|---|---|---|
|   |   |   |   | 1 | 2 | 3 |
| 4 | 5 | 6 | 7 | 8 | 9 | 10 |
| 11 | 12 | 13 | 14 | 15 | 16 | 17 |
| 18 | 19 | 20 | 21 | 22 | 23 | 24 |
| 25 | 26 | 27 | 28 | 29 | 30 | |

Wednesday **28**
Mittwoch
Mercredi
Mercoledì
Miércoles
Woensdag

Rosh Hashanah • Roch Hachana (begins at sundown)

**October 2011**

| S | M | T | W | T | F | S |
|---|---|---|---|---|---|---|
|   |   |   |   |   |   | 1 |
| 2 | 3 | 4 | 5 | 6 | 7 | 8 |
| 9 | 10 | 11 | 12 | 13 | 14 | 15 |
| 16 | 17 | 18 | 19 | 20 | 21 | 22 |
| 23 | 24 | 25 | 26 | 27 | 28 | 29 |
| 30 | 31 | | | | | |

Thursday **29**
Donnerstag
Jeudi
Giovedì
Jueves
Donderdag

Friday **30**
Freitag
Vendredi
Venerdì
Viernes
Vrijdag

**November 2011**

| S | M | T | W | T | F | S |
|---|---|---|---|---|---|---|
|   |   | 1 | 2 | 3 | 4 | 5 |
| 6 | 7 | 8 | 9 | 10 | 11 | 12 |
| 13 | 14 | 15 | 16 | 17 | 18 | 19 |
| 20 | 21 | 22 | 23 | 24 | 25 | 26 |
| 27 | 28 | 29 | 30 | | | |

Saturday **1**
Samstag
Samedi
Sabato
Sábado
Zaterdag

Sunday **2**
Sonntag
Dimanche
Domenica
Domingo
Zondag

Erntedankfest, *Germany*

Week 39

# October 2011 Oktober Octobre Ottobre Octubre Oktober

**3** Monday
Montag
Lundi
Lunedì
Lunes
Maandag

Tag der Deutschen Einheit, *Germany*

**4** Tuesday
Dienstag
Mardi
Martedì
Martes
Dinsdag

☽

**5** Wednesday
Mittwoch
Mercredi
Mercoledì
Miércoles
Woensdag

**6** Thursday
Donnerstag
Jeudi
Giovedì
Jueves
Donderdag

**7** Friday
Freitag
Vendredi
Venerdì
Viernes
Vrijdag

Yom Kippur • Yom Kippour (begins at sundown)

**8** Saturday
Samstag
Samedi
Sabato
Sábado
Zaterdag

**9** Sunday
Sonntag
Dimanche
Domenica
Domingo
Zondag

## September 2011

| S | M | T | W | T | F | S |
|---|---|---|---|---|---|---|
|   |   |   |   | 1 | 2 | 3 |
| 4 | 5 | 6 | 7 | 8 | 9 | 10 |
| 11 | 12 | 13 | 14 | 15 | 16 | 17 |
| 18 | 19 | 20 | 21 | 22 | 23 | 24 |
| 25 | 26 | 27 | 28 | 29 | 30 |   |

## October 2011

| S | M | T | W | T | F | S |
|---|---|---|---|---|---|---|
|   |   |   |   |   |   | 1 |
| 2 | 3 | 4 | 5 | 6 | 7 | 8 |
| 9 | 10 | 11 | 12 | 13 | 14 | 15 |
| 16 | 17 | 18 | 19 | 20 | 21 | 22 |
| 23 | 24 | 25 | 26 | 27 | 28 | 29 |
| 30 | 31 |   |   |   |   |   |

## November 2011

| S | M | T | W | T | F | S |
|---|---|---|---|---|---|---|
|   |   | 1 | 2 | 3 | 4 | 5 |
| 6 | 7 | 8 | 9 | 10 | 11 | 12 |
| 13 | 14 | 15 | 16 | 17 | 18 | 19 |
| 20 | 21 | 22 | 23 | 24 | 25 | 26 |
| 27 | 28 | 29 | 30 |   |   |   |

Week 40

# Oktober Octubre Ottobre Octobre Oktober October 2011

**Monday 10**
Montag
Lundi
Lunedì
Lunes
Maandag

Columbus Day, *USA*
Thanksgiving Day, *Canada*

**Tuesday 11**
Dienstag
Mardi
Martedì
Martes
Dinsdag

**Wednesday 12**
Mittwoch
Mercredi
Mercoledì
Miércoles ○
Woensdag

Sukkot • Souccot (begins at sundown)

**Thursday 13**
Donnerstag
Jeudi
Giovedì
Jueves
Donderdag

**Friday 14**
Freitag
Vendredi
Venerdì
Viernes
Vrijdag

**Saturday 15**
Samstag
Samedi
Sabato
Sábado
Zaterdag

**Sunday 16**
Sonntag
Dimanche
Domenica
Domingo
Zondag

### September 2011

| S | M | T | W | T | F | S |
|---|---|---|---|---|---|---|
| | | | | 1 | 2 | 3 |
| 4 | 5 | 6 | 7 | 8 | 9 | 10 |
| 11 | 12 | 13 | 14 | 15 | 16 | 17 |
| 18 | 19 | 20 | 21 | 22 | 23 | 24 |
| 25 | 26 | 27 | 28 | 29 | 30 | |

### October 2011

| S | M | T | W | T | F | S |
|---|---|---|---|---|---|---|
| | | | | | | 1 |
| 2 | 3 | 4 | 5 | 6 | 7 | 8 |
| 9 | 10 | 11 | 12 | 13 | 14 | 15 |
| 16 | 17 | 18 | 19 | 20 | 21 | 22 |
| 23 | 24 | 25 | 26 | 27 | 28 | 29 |
| 30 | 31 | | | | | |

### November 2011

| S | M | T | W | T | F | S |
|---|---|---|---|---|---|---|
| | | 1 | 2 | 3 | 4 | 5 |
| 6 | 7 | 8 | 9 | 10 | 11 | 12 |
| 13 | 14 | 15 | 16 | 17 | 18 | 19 |
| 20 | 21 | 22 | 23 | 24 | 25 | 26 |
| 27 | 28 | 29 | 30 | | | |

Week 41

# October 2011 Oktober Octobre Ottobre Octubre Oktober

**17** Monday
Montag
Lundi
Lunedì
Lunes
Maandag

### September 2011

| S | M | T | W | T | F | S |
|---|---|---|---|---|---|---|
|   |   |   |   | 1 | 2 | 3 |
| 4 | 5 | 6 | 7 | 8 | 9 | 10 |
| 11 | 12 | 13 | 14 | 15 | 16 | 17 |
| 18 | 19 | 20 | 21 | 22 | 23 | 24 |
| 25 | 26 | 27 | 28 | 29 | 30 |   |

**18** Tuesday
Dienstag
Mardi
Martedì
Martes
Dinsdag

### October 2011

| S | M | T | W | T | F | S |
|---|---|---|---|---|---|---|
|   |   |   |   |   |   | 1 |
| 2 | 3 | 4 | 5 | 6 | 7 | 8 |
| 9 | 10 | 11 | 12 | 13 | 14 | 15 |
| 16 | 17 | 18 | 19 | 20 | 21 | 22 |
| 23 | 24 | 25 | 26 | 27 | 28 | 29 |
| 30 | 31 |   |   |   |   |   |

**19** Wednesday
Mittwoch
Mercredi
Mercoledì
Miércoles
Woensdag

Shemini Atzeret (begins at sundown)

**20** Thursday
Donnerstag
Jeudi
Giovedì
Jueves     ☾
Donderdag

Simhat Torah (begins at sundown)

### November 2011

| S | M | T | W | T | F | S |
|---|---|---|---|---|---|---|
|   |   | 1 | 2 | 3 | 4 | 5 |
| 6 | 7 | 8 | 9 | 10 | 11 | 12 |
| 13 | 14 | 15 | 16 | 17 | 18 | 19 |
| 20 | 21 | 22 | 23 | 24 | 25 | 26 |
| 27 | 28 | 29 | 30 |   |   |   |

**21** Friday
Freitag
Vendredi
Venerdì
Viernes
Vrijdag

**22** Saturday
Samstag
Samedi
Sabato
Sábado
Zaterdag

**23** Sunday
Sonntag
Dimanche
Domenica
Domingo
Zondag

Week 42

"*Dad, can you read?*"

Monday **24**
Montag
Lundi
Lunedì
Lunes
Maandag

*Labour Day, New Zealand*

---

Tuesday **25**
Dienstag
Mardi
Martedì
Martes
Dinsdag

| **September 2011** | | | | | | |
|---|---|---|---|---|---|---|
| S | M | T | W | T | F | S |
| | | | | 1 | 2 | 3 |
| 4 | 5 | 6 | 7 | 8 | 9 | 10 |
| 11 | 12 | 13 | 14 | 15 | 16 | 17 |
| 18 | 19 | 20 | 21 | 22 | 23 | 24 |
| 25 | 26 | 27 | 28 | 29 | 30 | |

---

Wednesday **26**
Mittwoch
Mercredi
Mercoledì
Miércoles
Woensdag

*Nationalfeiertag, Austria*

| **October 2011** | | | | | | |
|---|---|---|---|---|---|---|
| S | M | T | W | T | F | S |
| | | | | | | 1 |
| 2 | 3 | 4 | 5 | 6 | 7 | 8 |
| 9 | 10 | 11 | 12 | 13 | 14 | 15 |
| 16 | 17 | 18 | 19 | 20 | 21 | 22 |
| 23 | 24 | 25 | 26 | 27 | 28 | 29 |
| 30 | 31 | | | | | |

---

Thursday **27**
Donnerstag
Jeudi
Giovedì
Jueves
Donderdag

---

Friday **28**
Freitag
Vendredi
Venerdì
Viernes
Vrijdag

| **November 2011** | | | | | | |
|---|---|---|---|---|---|---|
| S | M | T | W | T | F | S |
| | | 1 | 2 | 3 | 4 | 5 |
| 6 | 7 | 8 | 9 | 10 | 11 | 12 |
| 13 | 14 | 15 | 16 | 17 | 18 | 19 |
| 20 | 21 | 22 | 23 | 24 | 25 | 26 |
| 27 | 28 | 29 | 30 | | | |

---

Saturday **29**
Samstag
Samedi
Sabato
Sábado
Zaterdag

---

Sunday **30**
Sonntag
Dimanche
Domenica
Domingo
Zondag

*Clocks back one hour, UK*

*Einde Zomertijd, Belgium, Netherlands*
*Ende der Sommerzeit, Austria, Germany, Switzerland*

Week 43

# October 2011 Oktober Octobre Ottobre Octubre Oktober
# November 2011 November Novembre Novembre Noviembre November

**31** Monday
Montag
Lundi
Lunedì
Lunes — Reformationstag, *Germany*
Maandag
Halloween, *USA , UK*
Bank Holiday, *Rep. of Ireland*

**1** Tuesday
Dienstag
Mardi
Martedì
Martes
Dinsdag — All Saints' Day • Allerheiligen • Toussaint

**2** Wednesday
Mittwoch
Mercredi
Mercoledì
Miércoles
Woensdag — ☽
Allerseelen, *Austria*
Allerzielen, *Netherlands, Belgium*

**3** Thursday
Donnerstag
Jeudi
Giovedì
Jueves
Donderdag

**4** Friday
Freitag
Vendredi
Venerdì
Viernes
Vrijdag

**5** Saturday
Samstag
Samedi
Sabato
Sábado
Zaterdag

**6** Sunday
Sonntag
Dimanche
Domenica
Domingo
Zondag — Daylight Saving Time ends, *USA, Canada*

## October 2011

| S | M | T | W | T | F | S |
|---|---|---|---|---|---|---|
| | | | | | | 1 |
| 2 | 3 | 4 | 5 | 6 | 7 | 8 |
| 9 | 10 | 11 | 12 | 13 | 14 | 15 |
| 16 | 17 | 18 | 19 | 20 | 21 | 22 |
| 23 | 24 | 25 | 26 | 27 | 28 | 29 |
| 30 | 31 | | | | | |

## November 2011

| S | M | T | W | T | F | S |
|---|---|---|---|---|---|---|
| | | 1 | 2 | 3 | 4 | 5 |
| 6 | 7 | 8 | 9 | 10 | 11 | 12 |
| 13 | 14 | 15 | 16 | 17 | 18 | 19 |
| 20 | 21 | 22 | 23 | 24 | 25 | 26 |
| 27 | 28 | 29 | 30 | | | |

## December 2011

| S | M | T | W | T | F | S |
|---|---|---|---|---|---|---|
| | | | | 1 | 2 | 3 |
| 4 | 5 | 6 | 7 | 8 | 9 | 10 |
| 11 | 12 | 13 | 14 | 15 | 16 | 17 |
| 18 | 19 | 20 | 21 | 22 | 23 | 24 |
| 25 | 26 | 27 | 28 | 29 | 30 | 31 |

Week 44

Monday **7**
Montag
Lundi
Lunedì
Lunes
Maandag

Tuesday **8**
Dienstag
Mardi
Martedì
Martes
Dinsdag

| October 2011 | | | | | | |
|---|---|---|---|---|---|---|
| S | M | T | W | T | F | S |
| | | | | | | 1 |
| 2 | 3 | 4 | 5 | 6 | 7 | 8 |
| 9 | 10 | 11 | 12 | 13 | 14 | 15 |
| 16 | 17 | 18 | 19 | 20 | 21 | 22 |
| 23 | 24 | 25 | 26 | 27 | 28 | 29 |
| 30 | 31 | | | | | |

Wednesday **9**
Mittwoch
Mercredi
Mercoledì
Miércoles
Woensdag

| November 2011 | | | | | | |
|---|---|---|---|---|---|---|
| S | M | T | W | T | F | S |
| | | 1 | 2 | 3 | 4 | 5 |
| 6 | 7 | 8 | 9 | 10 | 11 | 12 |
| 13 | 14 | 15 | 16 | 17 | 18 | 19 |
| 20 | 21 | 22 | 23 | 24 | 25 | 26 |
| 27 | 28 | 29 | 30 | | | |

Thursday **10**
Donnerstag
Jeudi
Giovedì
Jueves
Donderdag

Friday **11**
Freitag
Vendredi
Venerdì
Viernes
Vrijdag

Martinstag, *Germany*
Armistice de 1918, *France*
Remembrance Day, *Canada, Australia*
Veteran's Day, *USA*
Wapenstilstand 1918, *Belgium*

| December 2011 | | | | | | |
|---|---|---|---|---|---|---|
| S | M | T | W | T | F | S |
| | | | | 1 | 2 | 3 |
| 4 | 5 | 6 | 7 | 8 | 9 | 10 |
| 11 | 12 | 13 | 14 | 15 | 16 | 17 |
| 18 | 19 | 20 | 21 | 22 | 23 | 24 |
| 25 | 26 | 27 | 28 | 29 | 30 | 31 |

Saturday **12**
Samstag
Samedi
Sabato
Sábado
Zaterdag

Sunday **13**
Sonntag
Dimanche
Domenica
Domingo
Zondag

Volkstrauertag, *Germany*
Remembrance Sunday, *UK*

Week 45

# November 2011 November Novembre Novembre Noviembre November

**14** Monday / Montag / Lundi / Lunedì / Lunes / Maandag

**October 2011**

| S | M | T | W | T | F | S |
|---|---|---|---|---|---|---|
| | | | | | | 1 |
| 2 | 3 | 4 | 5 | 6 | 7 | 8 |
| 9 | 10 | 11 | 12 | 13 | 14 | 15 |
| 16 | 17 | 18 | 19 | 20 | 21 | 22 |
| 23 | 24 | 25 | 26 | 27 | 28 | 29 |
| 30 | 31 | | | | | |

**15** Tuesday / Dienstag / Mardi / Martedì / Martes / Dinsdag

**16** Wednesday / Mittwoch / Mercredi / Mercoledì / Miércoles / Woensdag

Buß- und Bettag, *Germany*

**November 2011**

| S | M | T | W | T | F | S |
|---|---|---|---|---|---|---|
| | | 1 | 2 | 3 | 4 | 5 |
| 6 | 7 | 8 | 9 | 10 | 11 | 12 |
| 13 | 14 | 15 | 16 | 17 | 18 | 19 |
| 20 | 21 | 22 | 23 | 24 | 25 | 26 |
| 27 | 28 | 29 | 30 | | | |

**17** Thursday / Donnerstag / Jeudi / Giovedì / Jueves / Donderdag

**18** Friday / Freitag / Vendredi / Venerdì / Viernes / Vrijdag

**December 2011**

| S | M | T | W | T | F | S |
|---|---|---|---|---|---|---|
| | | | | 1 | 2 | 3 |
| 4 | 5 | 6 | 7 | 8 | 9 | 10 |
| 11 | 12 | 13 | 14 | 15 | 16 | 17 |
| 18 | 19 | 20 | 21 | 22 | 23 | 24 |
| 25 | 26 | 27 | 28 | 29 | 30 | 31 |

**19** Saturday / Samstag / Samedi / Sabato / Sábado / Zaterdag

**20** Sunday / Sonntag / Dimanche / Domenica / Domingo / Zondag

Totensonntag, *Germany*
Ewigkeitssonntag, *Austria*

Week 46

Monday **21**
Montag
Lundi
Lunedì
Lunes
Maandag

Tuesday **22**
Dienstag
Mardi
Martedì
Martes
Dinsdag

| October 2011 | | | | | | |
|---|---|---|---|---|---|---|
| S | M | T | W | T | F | S |
| | | | | | | 1 |
| 2 | 3 | 4 | 5 | 6 | 7 | 8 |
| 9 | 10 | 11 | 12 | 13 | 14 | 15 |
| 16 | 17 | 18 | 19 | 20 | 21 | 22 |
| 23 | 24 | 25 | 26 | 27 | 28 | 29 |
| 30 | 31 | | | | | |

Wednesday **23**
Mittwoch
Mercredi
Mercoledì
Miércoles
Woensdag

| November 2011 | | | | | | |
|---|---|---|---|---|---|---|
| S | M | T | W | T | F | S |
| | | 1 | 2 | 3 | 4 | 5 |
| 6 | 7 | 8 | 9 | 10 | 11 | 12 |
| 13 | 14 | 15 | 16 | 17 | 18 | 19 |
| 20 | 21 | 22 | 23 | 24 | 25 | 26 |
| 27 | 28 | 29 | 30 | | | |

Thursday **24**
Donnerstag
Jeudi
Giovedì
Jueves
Donderdag

Thanksgiving Day, USA

Friday **25**
Freitag
Vendredi
Venerdì
Viernes
Vrijdag

| December 2011 | | | | | | |
|---|---|---|---|---|---|---|
| S | M | T | W | T | F | S |
| | | | | 1 | 2 | 3 |
| 4 | 5 | 6 | 7 | 8 | 9 | 10 |
| 11 | 12 | 13 | 14 | 15 | 16 | 17 |
| 18 | 19 | 20 | 21 | 22 | 23 | 24 |
| 25 | 26 | 27 | 28 | 29 | 30 | 31 |

Saturday **26**
Samstag
Samedi
Sabato
Sábado
Zaterdag

Sunday **27**
Sonntag
Dimanche
Domenica
Domingo
Zondag

Week 47

# November 2011 November Novembre Novembre Noviembre November
# December 2011 Dezember Décembre Dicembre Diciembre December

**28** Monday
Montag
Lundi
Lunedì
Lunes
Maandag

## November 2011

| S | M | T | W | T | F | S |
|---|---|---|---|---|---|---|
|   |   | 1 | 2 | 3 | 4 | 5 |
| 6 | 7 | 8 | 9 | 10 | 11 | 12 |
| 13 | 14 | 15 | 16 | 17 | 18 | 19 |
| 20 | 21 | 22 | 23 | 24 | 25 | 26 |
| 27 | 28 | 29 | 30 |   |   |   |

**29** Tuesday
Dienstag
Mardi
Martedì
Martes
Dinsdag

## December 2011

| S | M | T | W | T | F | S |
|---|---|---|---|---|---|---|
|   |   |   |   | 1 | 2 | 3 |
| 4 | 5 | 6 | 7 | 8 | 9 | 10 |
| 11 | 12 | 13 | 14 | 15 | 16 | 17 |
| 18 | 19 | 20 | 21 | 22 | 23 | 24 |
| 25 | 26 | 27 | 28 | 29 | 30 | 31 |

**30** Wednesday
Mittwoch
Mercredi
Mercoledì
Miércoles
Woensdag

St. Andrew's Day, *Scotland*

## January 2012

| S | M | T | W | T | F | S |
|---|---|---|---|---|---|---|
| 1 | 2 | 3 | 4 | 5 | 6 | 7 |
| 8 | 9 | 10 | 11 | 12 | 13 | 14 |
| 15 | 16 | 17 | 18 | 19 | 20 | 21 |
| 22 | 23 | 24 | 25 | 26 | 27 | 28 |
| 29 | 30 | 31 |   |   |   |   |

**1** Thursday
Donnerstag
Jeudi
Giovedì
Jueves
Donderdag

**2** Friday
Freitag
Vendredi
Venerdì
Viernes
Vrijdag

☽

**3** Saturday
Samstag
Samedi
Sabato
Sábado
Zaterdag

**4** Sunday
Sonntag
Dimanche
Domenica
Domingo
Zondag

Week 48

"Shouldn't you be reading that to me out loud or something?"

*"Bad news, Dad—you're brain-dead!"*

# December Diciembre Dicembre Décembre Dezember December 2011

Monday **5**
Montag
Lundi
Lunedì
Lunes
Maandag

Sinterklaasavond, *Netherlands*

Tuesday **6**
Dienstag
Mardi
Martedì
Martes
Dinsdag

Saint-Nicolas, *France*
Sint Nicolaas, *Netherlands, Belgium*

Wednesday **7**
Mittwoch
Mercredi
Mercoledì
Miércoles
Woensdag

Thursday **8**
Donnerstag
Jeudi
Giovedì
Jueves
Donderdag

Immaculate Conception • Mariä Empfängnis • Immaculée Conception •
Maria onbevlekt ontvangen

Friday **9**
Freitag
Vendredi
Venerdì
Viernes
Vrijdag

Saturday **10**
Samstag
Samedi
Sabato
Sábado
Zaterdag

Sunday **11**
Sonntag
Dimanche
Domenica
Domingo
Zondag

## November 2011

| S | M | T | W | T | F | S |
|---|---|---|---|---|---|---|
|   |   | 1 | 2 | 3 | 4 | 5 |
| 6 | 7 | 8 | 9 | 10 | 11 | 12 |
| 13 | 14 | 15 | 16 | 17 | 18 | 19 |
| 20 | 21 | 22 | 23 | 24 | 25 | 26 |
| 27 | 28 | 29 | 30 |   |   |   |

## December 2011

| S | M | T | W | T | F | S |
|---|---|---|---|---|---|---|
|   |   |   |   | 1 | 2 | 3 |
| 4 | 5 | 6 | 7 | 8 | 9 | 10 |
| 11 | 12 | 13 | 14 | 15 | 16 | 17 |
| 18 | 19 | 20 | 21 | 22 | 23 | 24 |
| 25 | 26 | 27 | 28 | 29 | 30 | 31 |

## January 2012

| S | M | T | W | T | F | S |
|---|---|---|---|---|---|---|
| 1 | 2 | 3 | 4 | 5 | 6 | 7 |
| 8 | 9 | 10 | 11 | 12 | 13 | 14 |
| 15 | 16 | 17 | 18 | 19 | 20 | 21 |
| 22 | 23 | 24 | 25 | 26 | 27 | 28 |
| 29 | 30 | 31 |   |   |   |   |

Week 49

**12** Monday
Montag
Lundi
Lunedì
Lunes
Maandag

**November 2011**

| S | M | T | W | T | F | S |
|---|---|---|---|---|---|---|
|   |   | 1 | 2 | 3 | 4 | 5 |
| 6 | 7 | 8 | 9 | 10 | 11 | 12 |
| 13 | 14 | 15 | 16 | 17 | 18 | 19 |
| 20 | 21 | 22 | 23 | 24 | 25 | 26 |
| 27 | 28 | 29 | 30 |   |   |   |

**13** Tuesday
Dienstag
Mardi
Martedì
Martes
Dinsdag

**December 2011**

| S | M | T | W | T | F | S |
|---|---|---|---|---|---|---|
|   |   |   |   | 1 | 2 | 3 |
| 4 | 5 | 6 | 7 | 8 | 9 | 10 |
| 11 | 12 | 13 | 14 | 15 | 16 | 17 |
| 18 | 19 | 20 | 21 | 22 | 23 | 24 |
| 25 | 26 | 27 | 28 | 29 | 30 | 31 |

**14** Wednesday
Mittwoch
Mercredi
Mercoledì
Miércoles
Woensdag

**15** Thursday
Donnerstag
Jeudi
Giovedì
Jueves
Donderdag

**January 2012**

| S | M | T | W | T | F | S |
|---|---|---|---|---|---|---|
| 1 | 2 | 3 | 4 | 5 | 6 | 7 |
| 8 | 9 | 10 | 11 | 12 | 13 | 14 |
| 15 | 16 | 17 | 18 | 19 | 20 | 21 |
| 22 | 23 | 24 | 25 | 26 | 27 | 28 |
| 29 | 30 | 31 |   |   |   |   |

**16** Friday
Freitag
Vendredi
Venerdì
Viernes
Vrijdag

**17** Saturday
Samstag
Samedi
Sabato
Sábado
Zaterdag

**18** Sunday
Sonntag
Dimanche
Domenica
Domingo
Zondag

Week 50

Monday **19**
Montag
Lundi
Lunedì
Lunes
Maandag

Tuesday **20**
Dienstag
Mardi
Martedì
Martes
Dinsdag

Hanukkah • Hannoucah (begins at sundown)

Wednesday **21**
Mittwoch
Mercredi
Mercoledì
Miércoles
Woensdag

Thursday **22**
Donnerstag
Jeudi
Giovedì
Jueves
Donderdag

Winter Solstice • Wintersonnenwende • Solstice d'hiver (05:30 Universal Time)

Friday **23**
Freitag
Vendredi
Venerdì
Viernes
Vrijdag

Saturday **24**
Samstag
Samedi
Sabato
Sábado
Zaterdag

Christmas Eve • Heiligabend • Veille de Noël • Kerstavond

Sunday **25**
Sonntag
Dimanche
Domenica
Domingo
Zondag

Christmas Day • 1. Weihnachtslag • Noël • Eerste Kerstdag • Kerstmis

## November 2011

| S | M | T | W | T | F | S |
|---|---|---|---|---|---|---|
|   |   | 1 | 2 | 3 | 4 | 5 |
| 6 | 7 | 8 | 9 | 10 | 11 | 12 |
| 13 | 14 | 15 | 16 | 17 | 18 | 19 |
| 20 | 21 | 22 | 23 | 24 | 25 | 26 |
| 27 | 28 | 29 | 30 |   |   |   |

## December 2011

| S | M | T | W | T | F | S |
|---|---|---|---|---|---|---|
|   |   |   |   | 1 | 2 | 3 |
| 4 | 5 | 6 | 7 | 8 | 9 | 10 |
| 11 | 12 | 13 | 14 | 15 | 16 | 17 |
| 18 | 19 | 20 | 21 | 22 | 23 | 24 |
| 25 | 26 | 27 | 28 | 29 | 30 | 31 |

## January 2012

| S | M | T | W | T | F | S |
|---|---|---|---|---|---|---|
| 1 | 2 | 3 | 4 | 5 | 6 | 7 |
| 8 | 9 | 10 | 11 | 12 | 13 | 14 |
| 15 | 16 | 17 | 18 | 19 | 20 | 21 |
| 22 | 23 | 24 | 25 | 26 | 27 | 28 |
| 29 | 30 | 31 |   |   |   |   |

Week 51

# December 2011 Dezember Décembre Dicembre Diciembre December
# January 2012 Januar Janvier Gennaio Enero Januari

**26** Monday
Montag
Lundi
Lunedì
Lunes — Boxing Day, *Australia, New Zealand, Canada, UK*
Kwanzaa begins, *USA*
Maandag — St. Stephen's Day • Stephanitag • Stephanstag • 2. Weihnachtstag • Tweede Kerstdag
Bank Holiday, *UK*

---

## December 2011

| S | M | T | W | T | F | S |
|---|---|---|---|---|---|---|
|   |   |   |   | 1 | 2 | 3 |
| 4 | 5 | 6 | 7 | 8 | 9 | 10 |
| 11 | 12 | 13 | 14 | 15 | 16 | 17 |
| 18 | 19 | 20 | 21 | 22 | 23 | 24 |
| 25 | 26 | 27 | 28 | 29 | 30 | 31 |

**27** Tuesday
Dienstag
Mardi
Martedì
Martes
Dinsdag — Bank Holiday, *UK*

---

**28** Wednesday
Mittwoch
Mercredi
Mercoledì
Miércoles
Woensdag

---

## January 2012

| S | M | T | W | T | F | S |
|---|---|---|---|---|---|---|
| 1 | 2 | 3 | 4 | 5 | 6 | 7 |
| 8 | 9 | 10 | 11 | 12 | 13 | 14 |
| 15 | 16 | 17 | 18 | 19 | 20 | 21 |
| 22 | 23 | 24 | 25 | 26 | 27 | 28 |
| 29 | 30 | 31 |   |   |   |   |

**29** Thursday
Donnerstag
Jeudi
Giovedì
Jueves
Donderdag

---

**30** Friday
Freitag
Vendredi
Venerdì
Viernes
Vrijdag

---

## February 2012

| S | M | T | W | T | F | S |
|---|---|---|---|---|---|---|
|   |   |   | 1 | 2 | 3 | 4 |
| 5 | 6 | 7 | 8 | 9 | 10 | 11 |
| 12 | 13 | 14 | 15 | 16 | 17 | 18 |
| 19 | 20 | 21 | 22 | 23 | 24 | 25 |
| 26 | 27 | 28 | 29 |   |   |   |

**31** Saturday
Samstag
Samedi
Sabato
Sábado
Zaterdag — New Year's Eve • Silvester • Saint-Sylvestre • Oudejaarsdag • Oudejaarsavond

---

**1** Sunday
Sonntag
Dimanche
Domenica
Domingo — ☽
Zondag — Kwanzaa ends, *USA*
New Year's Day • Neujahr • Nouvel An • Nieuwjaar

Week 52

Monday
Montag
Lundi
Lunedì
Lunes
Maandag

**2**

Berchtoldstag, *Switzerland*
Bank Holiday, *UK, Scotland*

Tuesday
Dienstag
Mardi
Martedì
Martes
Dinsdag

**3**

| **December 2011** | | | | | | |
|---|---|---|---|---|---|---|
| S | M | T | W | T | F | S |
| | | | | 1 | 2 | 3 |
| 4 | 5 | 6 | 7 | 8 | 9 | 10 |
| 11 | 12 | 13 | 14 | 15 | 16 | 17 |
| 18 | 19 | 20 | 21 | 22 | 23 | 24 |
| 25 | 26 | 27 | 28 | 29 | 30 | 31 |

Wednesday
Mittwoch
Mercredi
Mercoledì
Miércoles
Woensdag

**4**

| **January 2012** | | | | | | |
|---|---|---|---|---|---|---|
| S | M | T | W | T | F | S |
| 1 | 2 | 3 | 4 | 5 | 6 | 7 |
| 8 | 9 | 10 | 11 | 12 | 13 | 14 |
| 15 | 16 | 17 | 18 | 19 | 20 | 21 |
| 22 | 23 | 24 | 25 | 26 | 27 | 28 |
| 29 | 30 | 31 | | | | |

Thursday
Donnerstag
Jeudi
Giovedì
Jueves
Donderdag

**5**

Friday
Freitag
Vendredi
Venerdì
Viernes
Vrijdag

**6**

| **February 2012** | | | | | | |
|---|---|---|---|---|---|---|
| S | M | T | W | T | F | S |
| | | | 1 | 2 | 3 | 4 |
| 5 | 6 | 7 | 8 | 9 | 10 | 11 |
| 12 | 13 | 14 | 15 | 16 | 17 | 18 |
| 19 | 20 | 21 | 22 | 23 | 24 | 25 |
| 26 | 27 | 28 | 29 | | | |

Epiphany • Heilige Drei Könige • Epiphanie • Driekoningen

Saturday
Samstag
Samedi
Sabato
Sábado
Zaterdag

**7**

Sunday
Sonntag
Dimanche
Domenica
Domingo
Zondag

**8**

Week 1

# January 2012 Januar Janvier Gennaio Enero Januari

| | | | | |
|---|---|---|---|---|
| **1 S** | | | 17 T | |
| 2 M | Week 1 | | 18 W | |
| 3 T | | | 19 T | |
| 4 W | | | 20 F | |
| 5 T | | | 21 S | |
| 6 F | | | **22 S** | |
| 7 S | | | 23 M | Week 4 |
| **8 S** | | | 24 T | |
| 9 M | Week 2 | | 25 W | |
| 10 T | | | 26 T | |
| 11 W | | | 27 F | |
| 12 T | | | 28 S | |
| 13 F | | | **29 S** | |
| 14 S | | | 30 M | Week 5 |
| **15 S** | | | 31 T | |
| 16 M | Week 3 | | | |

# February 2012 Februar Février Febbraio Febrero Februari

| | | | | |
|---|---|---|---|---|
| 1 W | | | 17 F | |
| 2 T | | | 18 S | |
| 3 F | | | **19 S** | |
| 4 S | | | 20 M | Week 8 |
| **5 S** | | | 21 T | |
| 6 M | Week 6 | | 22 W | |
| 7 T | | | 23 T | |
| 8 W | | | 24 F | |
| 9 T | | | 25 S | |
| 10 F | | | **26 S** | |
| 11 S | | | 27 M | Week 9 |
| **12 S** | | | 28 T | |
| 13 M | Week 7 | | 29 W | |
| 14 T | | | | |
| 15 W | | | | |
| 16 T | | | | |

## Maart Marzo Marzo Mars März **March 2012**

| | | | | |
|---|---|---|---|---|
| 1 T | | 17 S | | |
| 2 F | | **18 S** | | |
| 3 S | | 19 M | Week 12 | |
| **4 S** | | 20 T | | |
| 5 M | Week 10 | 21 W | | |
| 6 T | | 22 T | | |
| 7 W | | 23 F | | |
| 8 T | | 24 S | | |
| 9 F | | **25 S** | | |
| 10 S | | 26 M | Week 13 | |
| **11 S** | | 27 T | | |
| 12 M | Week 11 | 28 W | | |
| 13 T | | 29 T | | |
| 14 W | | 30 F | | |
| 15 T | | 31 S | | |
| 16 F | | | | |

## April Abril Aprile Avril April **April 2012**

| | | | | |
|---|---|---|---|---|
| **1 S** | | 17 T | | |
| 2 M | Week 14 | 18 W | | |
| 3 T | | 19 T | | |
| 4 W | | 20 F | | |
| 5 T | | 21 S | | |
| 6 F | | **22 S** | | |
| 7 S | | 23 M | Week 17 | |
| **8 S** | | 24 T | | |
| 9 M | Week 15 | 25 W | | |
| 10 T | | 26 T | | |
| 11 W | | 27 F | | |
| 12 T | | 28 S | | |
| 13 F | | **29 S** | | |
| 14 S | | 30 M | Week 18 | |
| **15 S** | | | | |
| 16 M | Week 16 | | | |

# May 2012 Mai Mai Maggio Mayo Mei

| | | | | |
|---|---|---|---|---|
| 1 T | | 17 T | |
| 2 W | | 18 F | |
| 3 T | | 19 S | |
| 4 F | | **20 S** | |
| 5 S | | 21 M | Week 21 |
| **6 S** | | 22 T | |
| 7 M | Week 19 | 23 W | |
| 8 T | | 24 T | |
| 9 W | | 25 F | |
| 10 T | | 26 S | |
| 11 F | | **27 S** | |
| 12 S | | 28 M | Week 22 |
| **13 S** | | 29 T | |
| 14 M | Week 20 | 30 W | |
| 15 T | | 31 T | |
| 16 W | | | |

# June 2012 Juni Juin Giugno Junio Juni

| | | | | |
|---|---|---|---|---|
| 1 F | | **17 S** | |
| 2 S | | 18 M | Week 25 |
| **3 S** | | 19 T | |
| 4 M | Week 23 | 20 W | |
| 5 T | | 21 T | |
| 6 W | | 22 F | |
| 7 T | | 23 S | |
| 8 F | | **24 S** | |
| 9 S | | 25 M | Week 26 |
| **10 S** | | 26 T | |
| 11 M | Week 24 | 27 W | |
| 12 T | | 28 T | |
| 13 W | | 29 F | |
| 14 T | | 30 S | |
| 15 F | | | |
| 16 S | | | |

# Juli Julio Luglio Juillet Juli July 2012

| | | | | | |
|---|---|---|---|---|---|
| **1 S** | | | 17 T | | |
| 2 M | Week 27 | | 18 W | | |
| 3 T | | | 19 T | | |
| 4 W | | | 20 F | | |
| 5 T | | | 21 S | | |
| 6 F | | | **22 S** | | |
| 7 S | | | 23 M | Week 30 | |
| **8 S** | | | 24 T | | |
| 9 M | Week 28 | | 25 W | | |
| 10 T | | | 26 T | | |
| 11 W | | | 27 F | | |
| 12 T | | | 28 S | | |
| 13 F | | | **29 S** | | |
| 14 S | | | 30 M | Week 31 | |
| **15 S** | | | 31 T | | |
| 16 M | Week 29 | | | | |

# Augustus Agosto Agosto Août August August 2012

| | | | | | |
|---|---|---|---|---|---|
| 1 W | | | 17 F | | |
| 2 T | | | 18 S | | |
| 3 F | | | **19 S** | | |
| 4 S | | | 20 M | Week 34 | |
| **5 S** | | | 21 T | | |
| 6 M | Week 32 | | 22 W | | |
| 7 T | | | 23 T | | |
| 8 W | | | 24 F | | |
| 9 T | | | 25 S | | |
| 10 F | | | **26 S** | | |
| 11 S | | | 27 M | Week 35 | |
| **12 S** | | | 28 T | | |
| 13 M | Week 33 | | 29 W | | |
| 14 T | | | 30 T | | |
| 15 W | | | 31 F | | |
| 16 T | | | | | |

## September 2012 September Septembre Settembre Septiembre September

| | | | | |
|---|---|---|---|---|
| 1 S | | 17 M | Week 38 |
| **2 S** | | 18 T | |
| 3 M | Week 36 | 19 W | |
| 4 T | | 20 T | |
| 5 W | | 21 F | |
| 6 T | | 22 S | |
| 7 F | | **23 S** | |
| 8 S | | 24 M | Week 39 |
| **9 S** | | 25 T | |
| 10 M | Week 37 | 26 W | |
| 11 T | | 27 T | |
| 12 W | | 28 F | |
| 13 T | | 29 S | |
| 14 F | | **30 S** | |
| 15 S | | | |
| **16 S** | | | |

## October 2012 Oktober Octobre Ottobre Octubre Oktober

| | | | | |
|---|---|---|---|---|
| 1 M | Week 40 | 17 W | |
| 2 T | | 18 T | |
| 3 W | | 19 F | |
| 4 T | | 20 S | |
| 5 F | | **21 S** | |
| 6 S | | 22 M | Week 43 |
| **7 S** | | 23 T | |
| 8 M | Week 41 | 24 W | |
| 9 T | | 25 T | |
| 10 W | | 26 F | |
| 11 T | | 27 S | |
| 12 F | | **28 S** | |
| 13 S | | 29 M | Week 44 |
| **14 S** | | 30 T | |
| 15 M | Week 42 | 31 W | |
| 16 T | | | |

# November Noviembre Novembre Novembre November **November 2012**

| | | | | |
|---|---|---|---|---|
| 1 T | | 17 S | | |
| 2 F | | **18 S** | | |
| 3 S | | 19 M | Week 47 | |
| **4 S** | | 20 T | | |
| 5 M | Week 45 | 21 W | | |
| 6 T | | 22 T | | |
| 7 W | | 23 F | | |
| 8 T | | 24 S | | |
| 9 F | | **25 S** | | |
| 10 S | | 26 M | Week 48 | |
| **11 S** | | 27 T | | |
| 12 M | Week 46 | 28 W | | |
| 13 T | | 29 T | | |
| 14 W | | 30 F | | |
| 15 T | | | | |
| 16 F | | | | |

# December Diciembre Dicembre Décembre Dezember **December 2012**

| | | | | |
|---|---|---|---|---|
| 1 S | | 17 M | Week 51 | |
| **2 S** | | 18 T | | |
| 3 M | Week 49 | 19 W | | |
| 4 T | | 20 T | | |
| 5 W | | 21 F | | |
| 6 T | | 22 S | | |
| 7 F | | **23 S** | | |
| 8 S | | 24 M | Week 52 | |
| **9 S** | | 25 T | | |
| 10 M | Week 50 | 26 W | | |
| 11 T | | 27 T | | |
| 12 W | | 28 F | | |
| 13 T | | 29 S | | |
| 14 F | | **30 S** | | |
| 15 S | | 31 M | Week 1 | |
| **16 S** | | | | |

# Addresses Adressen Adresses Indirizzi Direcciones Adressen

✉                              ☎ / @

✉                                    ✆/@

# Addresses Adressen Adresses Indirizzi Direcciones Adressen

✉                                    ☎/@

*"Dad, can you read?"*

www.teneues.com

$15.99 · C$18.99 · € 13,95
(Germany and Austria only -
Réservé à l'Allemagne et l'Autriche)
**Printed in China**
ISBN: 978-3-8327-**4265-2**

**teNeues**

9 783832 742652

Prints, T-shirts, and other products featuring these cartoons are available at newyorkerstore.com.